Illustrated ATLAS OF WORLD HISTORY

First American edition, 1992

Library of Congress Cataloging-in-Publication Data

Adams, Simon,
   Illustrated atlas of world history/Simon Adams, John Briquebec,
Ann Kramer.
      p.   cm.
   Contents: The ancient world—trade and religion—exploration
and empire—revolution and technology.
   Includes glossary, time line, and index.
   ISBN 0-679-82465-0 (pbk.)—ISBN 0-679-92465-5 (lib. bdg.)
   1. Historical geography—Maps. [1. Historical geography—Maps.
2. World history. 3. Atlases.] I. Briquebec, John. II. Kramer,
Ann.   III. Title
G1030.A33 1992 (G&M)
912—dc20   91-16652

Manufactured in Hong Kong 10 9 8 7 6 5 4 3 2 1

Map on cover courtesy of Andromeda (Oxford) Ltd.

A*Illustrated* TLAS OF WORLD HISTORY

Simon Adams   John Briquebec   Ann Kramer

Random House 🏠 New York

Contents

Introduction

This book tells the history of the world from the time when the very first peoples inhabited the earth some 300,000 years ago to the present day. It traces the rise of the world's first civilizations and the growth of different cultures around the world; it follows the development of religions, trade, industry, and technology through to our modern, fast-moving world.

The world has changed in many ways. Thousands of years ago different cultures arose in every part of the world. But they had little connection with each other as they were limited by the distance that people could travel. Gradually, civilizations made more and more contact with one another. Some flourished, some were destroyed, but over the years human history shifted from the story of separate civilizations to the history of one interconnected world.

This historical atlas is divided into four sections. "The Ancient World" describes how the earliest people emerged in Africa and spread to other areas, surviving by gathering food and hunting and gradually learning to use fire, to make tools, and then to farm. It tells how the first farmers settled in the Middle East, home of the first civilizations and cities. This section explores the great civilizations of Egypt, China, Greece, and Rome. It also describes the development of writing and language and the rise of the world's great religions.

"Trade and Religion" traces human history from A.D. 456 to 1450. It tells the story of the world from the fall of Rome to the beginning of the Reformation. It chronicles the breakup of the Roman and Chinese empires, the growth of the Byzantine empire, the rise of the great Islamic empire and culture, and the emergence of empires in America, Africa, and Asia. This section also examines the growth of cities and medieval culture in Europe as well as the course and impact of the Black Death.

"Exploration and Empire" looks at the history of the world from 1450 to 1760, from the Renaissance to the start of the Industrial Revolution. It explores the glittering Aztec and Inca civilizations, examines the great age of exploration, and traces the development of worldwide trade and its effects, the settlement of the Caribbean and the Americas, and the rise of empires in China and Japan. This section also looks at the development of printing, the history of slavery, and the growth of science.

Finally, "Revolution and Technology" tells the story of the modern world from the Industrial Revolution to the present day. It describes the impact of industrialism and the great social revolutions in North America, France, Russia, and China. It covers the two world wars and the years since 1945, including the Cold War, the rise of the nuclear age, and the growth of the environmental movement.

History is not just about dates and events. It is a story about people and how they have lived. This book takes a close look at the daily lives of people from the very beginning of history to the present. It includes special feature pages on the rise of religion, science, and technology; the development of language, printing, transportation, trade, and slavery; and the role of women. Using carefully chosen illustrations, maps, and photographs, the *Illustrated Atlas of World History* brings history to life in a colorful and exciting way. Difficult words in the text are highlighted in **bold** and explained in the glossary, while a time line at the end of the book provides a list of key dates.

THE ANCIENT WORLD

From the Earliest Civilizations to the Roman Empire

30,000 B.C.–A.D. 456

The Earth Is Peopled

History is what people write down about the past and the way in which it is interpreted. But to find out about life before written language was invented, about 5,000 years ago, we have to rely on **archaeology**, the study of what people leave behind them—their buildings, the tools they used, the clothes they wore, their pottery, and their paintings. Scientists can measure very accurately when objects were made and used, so we can learn a surprising amount about the **culture** of these long-dead people—that is, the way they lived, what they believed, and how they behaved.

Scientists called **anthropologists** use the remains of people themselves to show how humans developed from a group of mammals called **primates**, which also includes the great apes, gorillas, and chimpanzees. The earliest traces of **hominids**—people-like creatures—have been found in Africa and are given the scientific name *Australopithecus*, meaning "southern ape." The oldest-known fossil of *Australopithecus* was found in Ethiopia in 1981 and is four million years old. Modern people, whose scientific name is *Homo sapiens*, have existed for at least 300,000 years.

▲ Finding out about the past on a site in Peru. Archaeologists lay down a grid so that they can locate and record accurately any "finds" that they come across. In this way they can learn more about the people who made the things they discover.

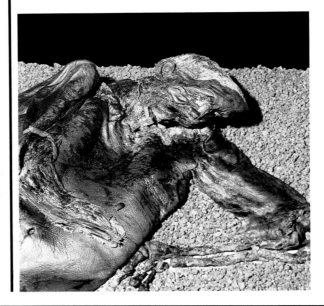

◀ When archaeologists dig up the remains of ancient humans they usually find only **fossilized** skeletons. But the body of this man was discovered at Lindow Moss in Cheshire, England, with the skin still intact, preserved by the bog in which he was found. He was murdered about 2,000 years ago, perhaps as a religious sacrifice.

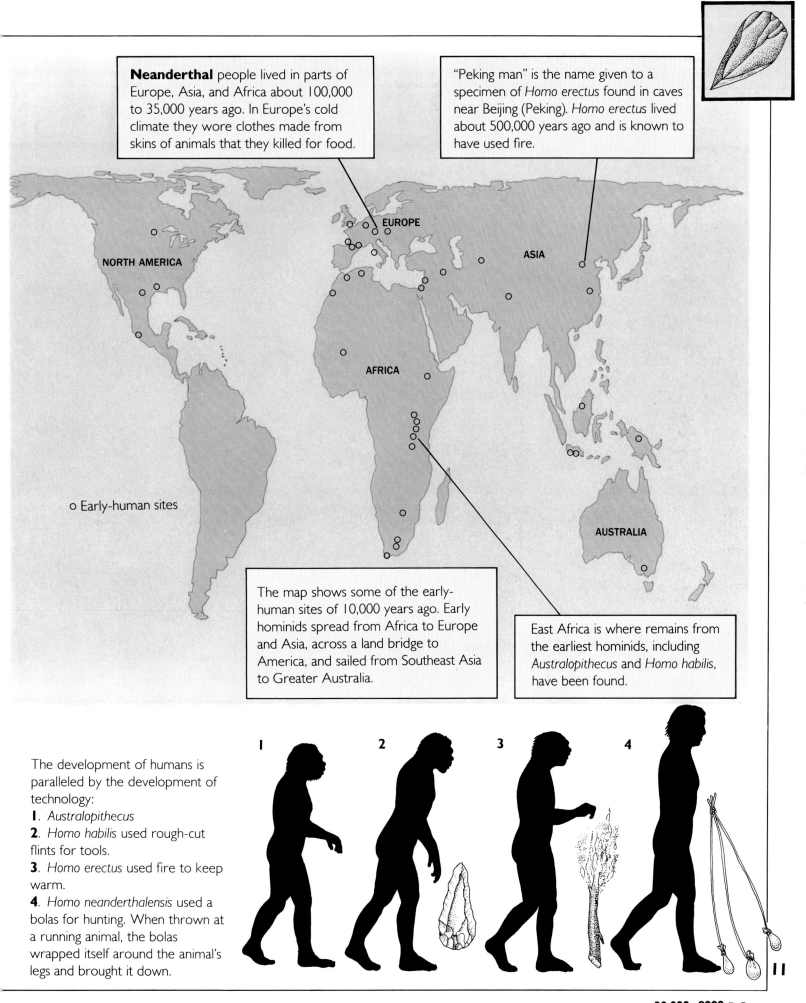

Neanderthal people lived in parts of Europe, Asia, and Africa about 100,000 to 35,000 years ago. In Europe's cold climate they wore clothes made from skins of animals that they killed for food.

"Peking man" is the name given to a specimen of *Homo erectus* found in caves near Beijing (Peking). *Homo erectus* lived about 500,000 years ago and is known to have used fire.

NORTH AMERICA

EUROPE

ASIA

AFRICA

AUSTRALIA

o Early-human sites

The map shows some of the early-human sites of 10,000 years ago. Early hominids spread from Africa to Europe and Asia, across a land bridge to America, and sailed from Southeast Asia to Greater Australia.

East Africa is where remains from the earliest hominids, including *Australopithecus* and *Homo habilis*, have been found.

The development of humans is paralleled by the development of technology:

1. *Australopithecus*

2. *Homo habilis* used rough-cut flints for tools.

3. *Homo erectus* used fire to keep warm.

4. *Homo neanderthalensis* used a bolas for hunting. When thrown at a running animal, the bolas wrapped itself around the animal's legs and brought it down.

11

The ice ages

The way in which people migrated (spread) around the world was affected by climate. The past million years have seen a series of **glacials** (ice ages) with warmer spells, called **interglacials**, in between. At the height of the glacials, ice sheets covered northern Europe, Asia, and North America and made it too cold for human settlement. But during the warmer interglacials people began to adapt slowly to the colder temperatures farther north by finding shelter and making fire, tools, and clothes. The first people to survive the colder climate of western Europe were the Neanderthals — so called because their remains were first found in the Neander Valley (*Tal*) in Germany. They lived between 100,000 and 35,000 years ago on areas of land bordering the great glaciers.

The ice that covered the land during the glacials took water from the seas and oceans, and as a result the sea level fell by many feet. This meant that land that had been covered by water was now exposed, and people could migrate across these **land bridges** to new areas. So the first people to reach America probably trekked from Siberia to Alaska about 40,000 years ago. In Southeast Asia people went, probably by raft, across what were then very shallow seas to New Guinea, and from there traveled on foot over a land bridge to Australia, where they settled at least 50,000 years ago.

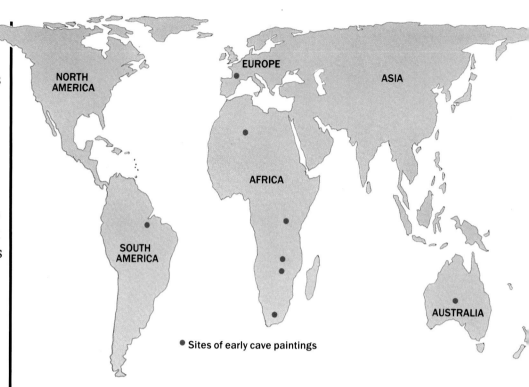

▲ The map shows where early cave and rock paintings have been found. *Homo sapiens* painted them between 35,000 and 10,000 years ago. The animal drawings may have been part of a magical ritual connected with hunting.

▼ Part of a wall painting discovered in a cave in Lascaux, France. The animals on this wall were painted between 19,000 and 18,000 years ago. The oxen have been drawn in black outline; the horses and deer have been filled in with a color.

12

▼ This carving of a female figure holding a bison's horn was found in a cave at Laussel, France. It is between 30,000 and 15,000 years old. Figures like this have been found in France and the Soviet Union. They are often called Venuses because they are thought to represent mother-goddesses.

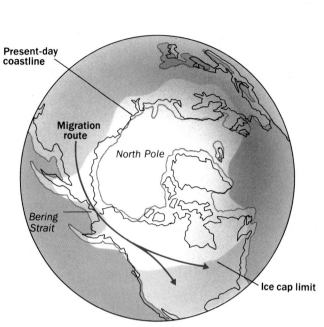

The map shows the southernmost limit reached by the ice cap in the last ice age (the Würm period). During the ice age a huge amount of water was frozen into the ice cap: in places the ice cap was 10,000 feet thick. As a result the level of the world's oceans fell by more than 300 feet, and there were land bridges in many places where there is now sea. Animals migrated across these land bridges, followed by the humans who hunted them. In this way early humans reached America.

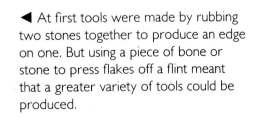

◀ At first tools were made by rubbing two stones together to produce an edge on one. But using a piece of bone or stone to press flakes off a flint meant that a greater variety of tools could be produced.

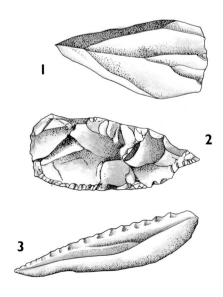

1. A knifelike blade
2. A borer
3. A point

13

The Fertile Crescent and Its Neighbors

The hunter-gatherers

The people who roamed the earth 500,000 years ago hunted animals and gathered whatever nuts, fruits, and other vegetable matter they could find for food. When the supply of food in one place ran out, or when the herds of animals moved on, the people had to move too. Collecting or catching enough food to stay alive took up everybody's time.

The first farmers

What changed people's lives, over many generations, was the gradual development of **agriculture**. Slowly, people discovered that certain plants could be cultivated, or grown, to provide crops, and certain animals could be domesticated, or raised, to provide meat, milk, hides, or wool. Gradually, many people began to rely on the steady supply of food from their crops and animals, and instead of moving from place to place to gather their food, they started to settle in fertile areas of land.

Nearly 10,000 years ago, some of the earliest farmers settled in what is often called the Fertile Crescent. This is an area of land that is well watered by the Tigris, Euphrates, and Nile rivers. Here people grew wild wheat and wild barley and kept goats, sheep, pigs, and cattle.

▲ Without water, crops cannot grow, so a system of watering cultivated land, or **irrigation**, is very important. Different methods were used by different peoples. In this picture the ox is turning a wheel to raise pots of water from a larger channel to a smaller one.

▶ The goat was one of the first animals to be domesticated and kept for its milk.

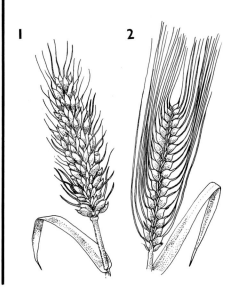

◀ The first grains to be cultivated were various types of wheat (**1**) and barley (**2**). The early farmers harvested wild grains and then sowed (planted) the seeds they obtained, watering them and fertilizing them to give fatter seed grains.

8000–300 B.C.

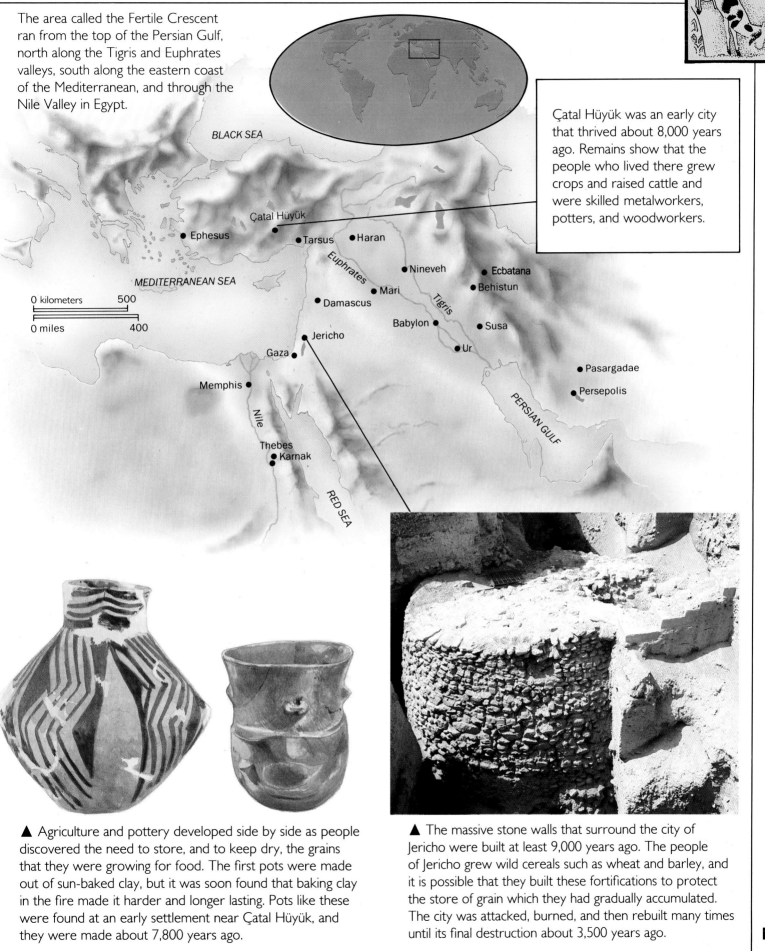

The area called the Fertile Crescent ran from the top of the Persian Gulf, north along the Tigris and Euphrates valleys, south along the eastern coast of the Mediterranean, and through the Nile Valley in Egypt.

BLACK SEA

MEDITERRANEAN SEA

0 kilometers   500
0 miles   400

Ephesus
Çatal Hüyük
Tarsus
Haran
Euphrates
Nineveh
Ecbatana
Behistun
Mari
Damascus
Tigris
Babylon
Susa
Jericho
Ur
Gaza
Pasargadae
Memphis
Persepolis
Nile
PERSIAN GULF
Thebes
Karnak
RED SEA

Çatal Hüyük was an early city that thrived about 8,000 years ago. Remains show that the people who lived there grew crops and raised cattle and were skilled metalworkers, potters, and woodworkers.

▲ Agriculture and pottery developed side by side as people discovered the need to store, and to keep dry, the grains that they were growing for food. The first pots were made out of sun-baked clay, but it was soon found that baking clay in the fire made it harder and longer lasting. Pots like these were found at an early settlement near Çatal Hüyük, and they were made about 7,800 years ago.

▲ The massive stone walls that surround the city of Jericho were built at least 9,000 years ago. The people of Jericho grew wild cereals such as wheat and barley, and it is possible that they built these fortifications to protect the store of grain which they had gradually accumulated. The city was attacked, burned, and then rebuilt many times until its final destruction about 3,500 years ago.

The first civilizations

After many generations settlements grew and became established. In some areas people began to coordinate and organize their beliefs, their government, and their **trade**. As a result, the first **civilizations** emerged.

The earliest civilizations of the Fertile Crescent were in Mesopotamia, the land between the Tigris and the Euphrates rivers. The first people to settle in Mesopotamia were the Sumerians. After about 3500 B.C. they established centers of civilization in towns and cities, called "**city-states**." In each of these city-states was a royal palace, a temple tower (**ziggurat**), and an administrative center, around which were houses, and beyond them the fields and marshlands of the farmers. One of these city-states, Ur, became very powerful because of its trade: cloth were produced in the city's workshops and exchanged for copper, gold, ivory, and timber.

Around 2000 B.C. the power of Ur was weakened, and a **nomadic** people from the north, the Amorites, took over the land where the Tigris and the Euphrates converge and established a center called Babylon in the kingdom of Babylonia. But the kingdom was conquered by the Assyrians, a warlike nation from the city-state of Assur, with a trained and organized army and weapons made from **bronze** and iron.

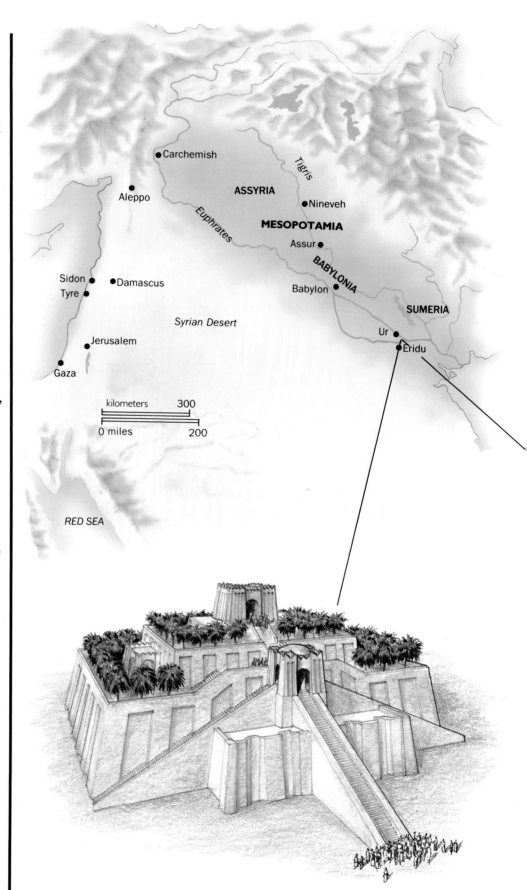

▲ A drawing of the ziggurat at Ur. On the top was a temple where the king performed religious rites and sacrifices with the high priestess of Ur. It was built of sun-baked clay bricks and it may have been decorated with glazed tiles (not shown here). It was finished in about 2100 B.C.

16

▲ A picture of the impression from a limestone cylinder **seal** made in Mesopotamia between 5,500 and 5,000 years ago. Seals were used to identify property. The upper part of the impression shows some cattle; below is a cowshed.

▲ The Marsh Arabs of southern Iraq still build and live in reed houses, just as the farmers in the marshlands of Mesopotamia did. The houses are similar in construction to the cowshed shown on the seal (*above left*).

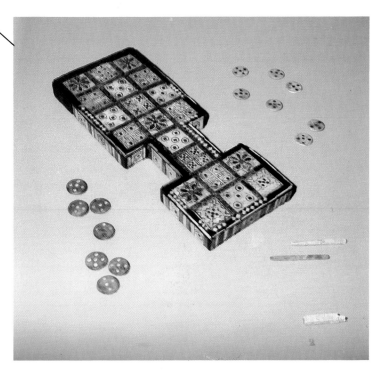

▲ A board game, complete with dice and counters, made and used in Ur about 4,500 years ago. The Mesopotamians were skilled mathematicians; from them we inherit the method of dividing up time into 60 seconds, minutes, and hours, and a circle into 360 degrees.

Mesopotamia
*c.*8000 B.C.: first development of agriculture.
*c.*3500 B.C.: the Sumerians begin to develop their civilization.
*c.*3200 B.C.: earliest writing.
*c.*2800 B.C.: the first Semitic people settle in Mesopotamia.
2360 B.C.: Akkadian Empire founded by Sargon.
1792–1750 B.C.: rule of Hammurabi, king of Babylon.
*c.*1750 B.C.: rise of Babylonian Empire.
*c.*721–705 B.C.: Assyrian Empire at height of its power.
689 B.C.: Babylon destroyed by Assyrians.
539 B.C.: Nabonidus, last king of Babylonia, surrenders to Cyrus the Great of Persia.

17

The ancient Egyptians

Like the people of Mesopotamia, the ancient Egyptians established their settlements on fertile land along the Nile River, more than 5,000 years ago. There were two **kingdoms**—Lower Egypt in the delta area at the mouth of the Nile and Upper Egypt in the south, but these were united in around 3200 B.C. by the **pharaoh** (king) Menes, who was the first in a line of pharaohs who ruled Egypt for the next 2,500 years. Whereas the various kingdoms of Mesopotamia, based around city-states, remained relatively small, the kingdom of Egypt flourished under one rule, with a single system governing the whole land.

Heading the system was the pharaoh. Considered to be a god, he commanded the service and goods of all his subjects. The belief that, as gods, the pharaohs continued to live after death led to the building of the pyramids. In these huge tombs the pharaohs were buried with everything they might need in the afterlife, including servants and spouses. The immense power that the pharaohs wielded over their people is shown by the time, the number of workers, and the wealth needed to build these tombs.

Egyptian farmers

At the other end of the social system were the peasant farmers who worked in the fields. Egyptian agriculture relied on the annual flooding of the Nile River, which left

continued on p. 20

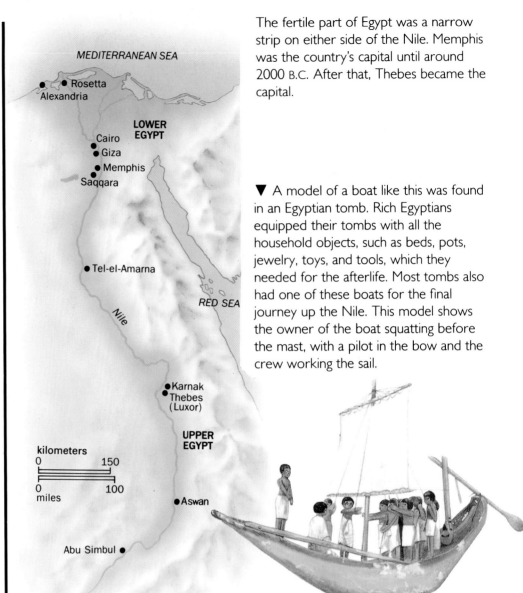

The fertile part of Egypt was a narrow strip on either side of the Nile. Memphis was the country's capital until around 2000 B.C. After that, Thebes became the capital.

▼ A model of a boat like this was found in an Egyptian tomb. Rich Egyptians equipped their tombs with all the household objects, such as beds, pots, jewelry, toys, and tools, which they needed for the afterlife. Most tombs also had one of these boats for the final journey up the Nile. This model shows the owner of the boat squatting before the mast, with a pilot in the bow and the crew working the sail.

▼ A section through the Great Pyramid at Giza, near Cairo, the largest of the pyramids. It was constructed with 2,300,000 blocks of stone, each weighing an average of 2½ tons. Some of the stone was dug up nearby; some was brought by river from Aswan and dragged on rollers from the river's edge. The ancient Greek historian Herodotus recorded that 100,000 people toiled for 20 years to build this pyramid as a tomb for Pharaoh Khufu, who died in 2567 B.C.

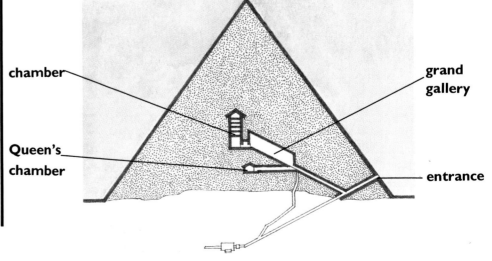

8000–300 B.C.

▲ A wall painting from the tomb of Menna at Thebes.

▲ Scenes from a modern reconstruction of an ancient Egyptian village. The ordinary people who worked in the fields were often paid barely more than they needed to live on, and a large percentage of the harvest was taken away in tax.

Top: Trampled ears of grain are picked up in flat wooden scoops and tossed high into the air to separate the chaff (which blows away) from the wheat (which falls to the ground), a process called winnowing.

Below: Harvested grain is carried from the field in large baskets.

▶ Egyptian men wore a simple linen kilt knotted around the waist. It was sometimes decorated with pleating at the front. Official and ceremonial dress was more complicated—for example, priests wore leopard skins.

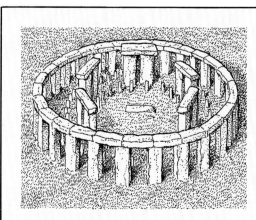

Did you know that Stonehenge in England was begun at about the same time as the Great Pyramid in Egypt?

19

behind it fertile silt in which crops such as wheat, barley, and flax could be grown. Wheat and barley were used to make bread and beer, and flax provided the linen with which the Egyptians made most of their clothes. Meat was a luxury for most ancient Egyptians, but cattle were reared for their dairy produce, as beasts of burden, and for slaughter in religious rituals.

Egyptian people
In between these two extremes were many levels of Egyptian society, such as the **viziers** and supervisors, who were close to the pharaoh at court, priests in the temples, merchants, and craftspeople. Scribes were particularly important because they oversaw the harvest and recorded the yield of the crops; they also wrote down the history of their times and inscriptions glorifying Egyptian victories in war.

The population of ancient Egypt was spread among the towns and small villages along the Nile. The most important settlements were the royal cities chosen by the pharaohs, such as Memphis and Thebes. Next in importance were the nome (provinces), which were local centers for administration and taxation.

The buildings, except of course the pyramids and some of the temples that were built of stone, were made of unbaked mud brick — a mixture of Nile mud and straw, shaped in wooden molds and left to dry in the sun.

▲ The Egyptians worshiped many gods and goddesses, and they also believed in magic to guard against evil. This is a drawing of a magic wand, made from hippopotamus ivory, that was used to protect the owner against poisonous creatures, such as snakes.

◄ When a pharaoh died, his body was preserved by a process called mummification so he could continue on his journey in the afterlife. The body was wrapped in bandages and enclosed in a highly decorated mummy case like the one shown here. Later, wealthy Egyptians also received this treatment.

▼ This picture of a tomb model of a man shows him filtering a fermented mixture to make beer. Beer was the main drink in Egypt. It was made from barley and stored in beer jars.

The Spread of Writing

As civilizations emerged and trade developed, people began to record information by writing it down. The first writing we know of comes from Mesopotamia as early as 3200 B.C. Here the Sumerians drew little pictures on clay tablets, probably in order to keep records and accounts of their goods for trading. Gradually over the next 200 years these "pictograms" were replaced by patterns made by a chopped-off reed on soft clay: each pattern stood for a sound or syllable. This type of writing is called cuneiform (meaning wedge-shaped). It lasted from about 3000 B.C. to A.D. 75, several centuries longer than our own writing has been in use!

Although they knew of cuneiform, the Egyptians developed their own more elaborate picture writing called **hieroglyphics**. Like the Sumerians, the Egyptians gradually developed a system in which their pictograms, or hieroglyphics, stood for sounds rather than things. However, the Egyptians also invented a new and more convenient material on which to write—sheets of papyrus made from the papyrus reed, from which comes our word "paper."

The first surviving specimens of Chinese writing were found on the **oracle** bones of the Shang dynasty (*see page 26*). Over 2,000 different characters have been found on these bones, and it is obvious that writing was already well developed in China by this time. The Chinese language developed in a completely different way from the Western languages, using the shapes of characters to represent things and ideas, not syllables or sounds.

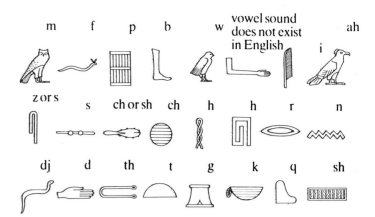

▲ Egyptian hieroglyphs: some of the signs have the value of one letter of our alphabet, others represent two letters or more.

▲ Writing on a soft clay tablet with a reed pen.

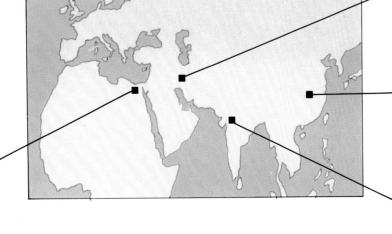

Egyptian hieroglyphs

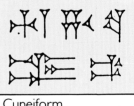

Cuneiform

Chinese characters

Indus Valley glyphs

The Persians

The last of the early civilizations of this region was in Persia (Iran). About 2,900 years ago two nomadic tribes, the Medes and the Persians, moved southward from the area that is now the southern Soviet Union. In 549 B.C. a Persian king, Cyrus the Great, conquered the Medes and set about creating a huge **empire**. The Persians were good riders, and they used iron weapons. Within only 30 years they had expanded their empire to cover the whole of Mesopotamia, Anatolia (Turkey), the eastern Mediterranean, and what are now Pakistan and Afghanistan.

However, it was left to a later Persian king, Darius I, to devise a system of government that would hold together this huge empire. Darius divided the Empire into 23 (later 31) administrative regions, called **satrapies**, each with a governor (satrap) who controlled a region but who also had to make gifts of cereals and other produce to the Persian king. Roads were built, including the Royal Road, to link together the various parts of the Empire. They were also used for trade — traders transported and sold raw materials, clothes, carpets, and spices. In 520 B.C. Darius introduced a standardized currency to be used throughout the Empire, which also encouraged trade.

The Persian Empire flourished until 331 B.C., when it was conquered by Alexander the Great of Macedonia.

▲ This tiny gold model of a Persian chariot is part of the "Oxus treasure" found in Afghanistan. It shows the kind of vehicle in which Persian nobles traveled on business along the roads of the Empire. The Persians were skilled craftspeople, renowned for their fine work in gold and silver.

Both these impressions are like those taken from seals that were rolled across moist clay to produce signatures to identify property.

▲ A seal like this was probably the property of one of Darius's highest officials, and shows the king in his chariot, hunting lions.

◄ The ordinary people of the Empire rarely appeared on seals, but this one shows a man plowing with his team of oxen.

22

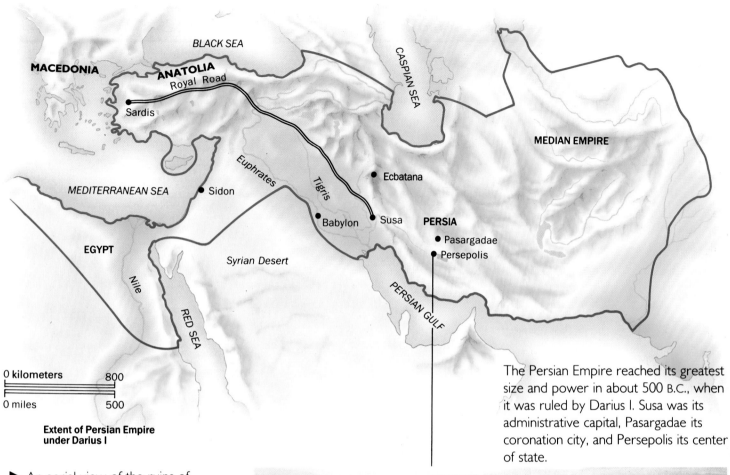

BLACK SEA

MACEDONIA

ANATOLIA
Royal Road

Sardis

CASPIAN SEA

MEDIAN EMPIRE

Ecbatana

MEDITERRANEAN SEA

Sidon

Euphrates

Tigris

Babylon

Susa

PERSIA

Pasargadae

Persepolis

EGYPT

Nile

Syrian Desert

RED SEA

PERSIAN GULF

0 kilometers 800

0 miles 500

**Extent of Persian Empire
under Darius I**

The Persian Empire reached its greatest size and power in about 500 B.C., when it was ruled by Darius I. Susa was its administrative capital, Pasargadae its coronation city, and Persepolis its center of state.

▶ An aerial view of the ruins of Persepolis as they stand today in southern Iran. Darius I ordered the start of building work in 520 B.C. Persepolis was only used by the "King of Kings" and his court once a year during New Year's, when tribute was brought to him by the peoples of his Empire.

▶ A relief sculpture showing Assyrians bearing tribute to the "King of Kings" at the New Year's ceremony. They bring dressed animal skins and a pair of rams chosen from their flocks.

Civilizations of Eastern and Southern Asia

Ancient China

The earliest civilizations of ancient China grew up on the banks of its three largest rivers: the Huang He (Yellow River), the Chang Jiang (Yangtze), and the Xi Jiang (West River). Like the peoples of the Fertile Crescent, the Chinese farmers relied on the rivers for water to grow their crops, but devastating floods were always a threat. There was also the danger of invasion by the Xiung-Nu (Huns and Mongols). As a result, the building of systems of waterworks and of barriers against human attacks were important aspects of China's early history.

The Shang

The first documented **dynasty**, or ruling family, was called the Shang. Their capital city seems to have been moved—maybe as a result of both floods and invasions. However, excavations at one of the cities, An-yang, revealed wooden houses in which most people lived, as well as palaces, storerooms, and tombs of the kings and people of rank.

People of the Shang dynasty grew millet, wheat, and some rice and kept domesticated animals such as cattle, pigs, sheep, dogs, and chickens. Silk was already a valued cloth, but it was worn only by the rich—

continued on p. 26

▲ A drawing of an early Chinese house of about 2000 B.C. It probably held one family. The roof was supported by wooden uprights. Traces of such uprights have been found by archaeologists excavating sites near the Huang He (Yellow River) in northern China.

► A drawing of a pottery model of a watchtower made around A.D. 100. This model was made for the tomb of a wealthy person in the Han period.

Ancient China
c.1766–c.1122 B.C.: Shang dynasty (Bronze Age culture).
c.1122–c.221 B.C.: Chou dynasty.
c.650 B.C.: introduction of ironworking.
551 B.C.: Confucius born.
221–206 B.C.: Ch'in dynasty (first united empire).
202 B.C.–A.D. 220: Han dynasty (rise of Confucianism).
c.112 B.C.: opening of "Silk Road" linking China to the West.
50 B.C.–A.D. 50: Buddhism introduced from India.
A.D. 220–581: Six dynasties period.

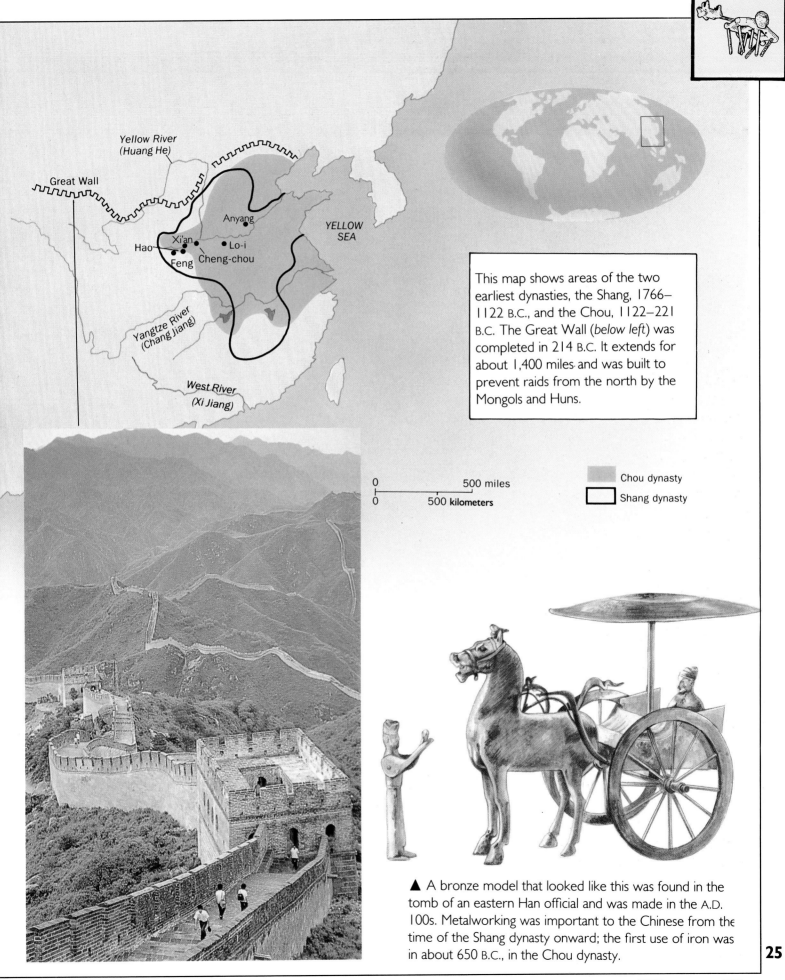

Yellow River
(Huang He)

Great Wall

Anyang

Xi'an

Hao

Lo-i

Feng

Cheng-chou

YELLOW
SEA

Yangtze River
(Chang Jiang)

West River
(Xi Jiang)

This map shows areas of the two earliest dynasties, the Shang, 1766–1122 B.C., and the Chou, 1122–221 B.C. The Great Wall (*below left*) was completed in 214 B.C. It extends for about 1,400 miles and was built to prevent raids from the north by the Mongols and Huns.

0   500 miles

0   500 **kilometers**

Chou dynasty

Shang dynasty

▲ A bronze model that looked like this was found in the tomb of an eastern Han official and was made in the A.D. 100s. Metalworking was important to the Chinese from the time of the Shang dynasty onward; the first use of iron was in about 650 B.C., in the Chou dynasty.

25

ordinary people wore linen or cotton.

The dynasty came to an end when nomadic groups from the west took over, establishing the Chou dynasty. In about 650 B.C. the Chou introduced iron working. Previously the Shang had used metal—usually bronze—only for ornamental purposes, but now iron was used for weapons and for agricultural tools such as plows. This made cultivation much easier.

The Ch'in dynasty
In 221 B.C. a Ch'in king, Shih Huang Ti, pronounced himself emperor and founded the Ch'in dynasty. He unified his vast empire by standardizing weights and measures, introducing a uniform currency, and by improving the network of roads and canals.

About fifteen years later, the Ch'in dynasty was succeeded by the Han dynasty, which ruled—with a short interruption—until A.D. 220.

Japan
The development of civilizations was slower in Japan, mainly because of this island country's isolation. Fishing provided much of the food needed, and the early Japanese, the Jōmon, also cultivated grains, such as rice, and kept domestic animals. After about 200 B.C. the Yayoi culture arose. Its people used bronze and iron to make decorative objects, but still used stone knives and simple wooden containers.

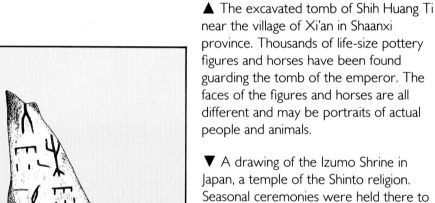

▲ The excavated tomb of Shih Huang Ti near the village of Xi'an in Shaanxi province. Thousands of life-size pottery figures and horses have been found guarding the tomb of the emperor. The faces of the figures and horses are all different and may be portraits of actual people and animals.

▼ A drawing of the Izumo Shrine in Japan, a temple of the Shinto religion. Seasonal ceremonies were held there to ensure good crops, fertility, and health.

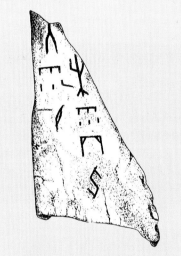

Did you know that since ancient times the Chinese have used bones as oracles to try to foretell the future? Questions to the gods were carved onto the bones. When the bones were heated, cracks appeared across the written characters and gave the gods' answers.

26

Religions and Beliefs in Eastern Asia

Three of the world's main religions and beliefs began in eastern Asia: Hinduism, Buddhism, and Confucianism.

Hinduism

Hinduism is the world's oldest surviving religion and is still the main religion of India. It is not known exactly when and where it began, but the origins of Hinduism lie in the religion of the Aryan people who settled northern India from 1500 B.C. onward.

Archaeologists know little about these people, but what they do know has been learned from their literature, which was passed down by word of mouth for many centuries. The most important early work of this literature was the *Rig-Veda*, which became a holy book for all Hindus. The *Rig-Veda* is a collection of hymns which were originally chanted by the Brahmans, or priests, at sacrifices. It was not written down until A.D. 1300.

The three most important Hindu gods are Brahma, creator of the universe, Vishnu, who preserves the universe, and Shiva, who destroys it.

Buddhism

Buddhism also originated in northern India. It was founded by a prince named Siddhartha Gautama, who was born about 563 B.C. to a life of wealth and luxury. When he was 29 he left his family and rejected his comfortable life. Dressed like a beggar, he wandered from place to place. He began exploring the traditional teachings of the Hindu Brahmans, but he rejected their

ritual and sacrifice and instead began to teach a method of disciplining both mind and body in order to attain Nirvana, a state of perfect peace and happiness. He was called Buddha, "the Enlightened One."

Confucianism

Confucianism is a way of life and moral behavior rather than a religion. It is based on the teachings of a Chinese wise man who lived from 551 to 479 B.C. He was named K'ung Fu-tzu, which was translated into Latin as Confucius. As a young man he worked as an administrator for a prince, but he withdrew from

▼ There are many statues and carvings of the Buddha, but none are from his own time.

active life and began to meditate on questions of right and wrong. His "system" was that people's lives should be ruled by a principle of order: doing good meant finding your place in that order and respecting the places of other people and things in it.

The teachings of Confucius were adopted by the rulers of the Chinese empire as the official philosophy; they also spread to Korea and Japan.

The traditional religion of Japan is Shinto, which is more than 2,500 years old.

▲ The teachings of Confucius influenced the development of Chinese civilization for two thousand years.

The Indus Valley civilizations

The early peoples of the Indian subcontinent inhabited sites around the Indus and Ganges rivers, but the first civilization to emerge was in the Indus Valley in about 2500 B.C.

The two largest cities of the Indus Valley civilization were Mohenjo-Daro and Harappa. At the center of each was an artificial mound, or **citadel**, with a large well-ventilated granary in which grain was stored. At Mohenjo-Daro there was also a bathhouse, with cells and private baths surrounding a large bath which may have been used by priests. Beyond the citadel the workers' houses were built in well-planned rows, with a system of drains and sewers. The houses had several rooms, a well, and a toilet and were built around a courtyard. All of the buildings were made with bricks baked in wood-fired ovens.

The huge granaries at Harappa and Mohenjo-Daro suggest that the livelihood of the Indus Valley people was based on farming—wheat and barley were the main crops. They also traded goods, such as cotton, probably with the peoples farther west in Mesopotamia.

The Indus civilization seems to have ended quite suddenly in about 1500 B.C., possibly when its cities were attacked by **Aryan** invaders from the northwest. No single civilization took its place until the Mauryan Empire emerged in central India in about 320 B.C.

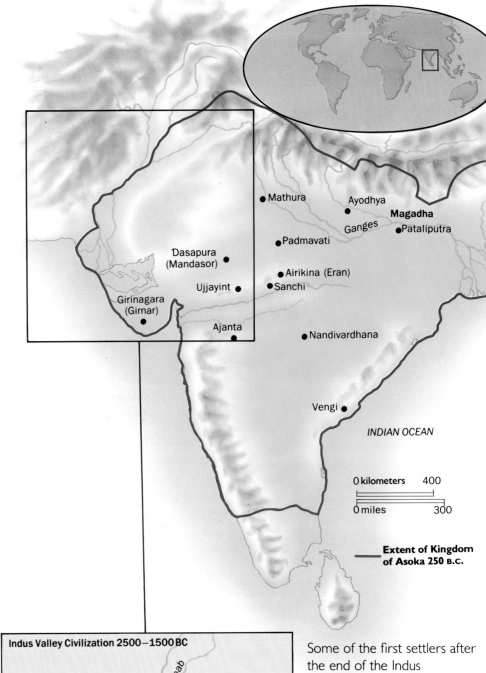

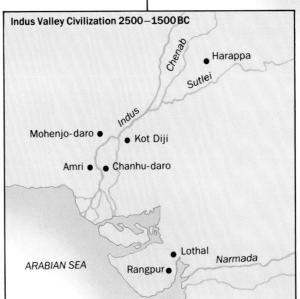

Indus Valley Civilization 2500–1500 BC

Some of the first settlers after the end of the Indus civilization were the Aryans from the northwest, who established themselves along the valley of the Ganges River. By the 500s B.C. great cities had grown up. They were often at war with one another, but one center, Magadha, emerged as more powerful than the rest. Later this kingdom came under the rule of the Mauryan Empire, which united nearly all of India under its greatest emperor, Asoka (273–232 B.C.).

► The impressive ruins of the city of Mohenjo-Daro. The buildings were carefully planned on a grid design and built with **kiln**-baked bricks. These bricks were of such good quality that many of them were taken away and used in the A.D. 1800s to build railway embankments.

▼ Brick-lined shafts like this are found in the courtyards of many of the houses in Mohenjo-Daro. They may have been wells or storage places for vases or jars.

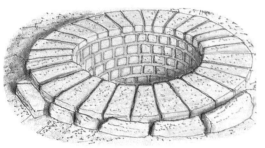

▼ Over 1,200 of these seals have been found in the ruins of Mohenjo-Daro. They were used by merchants to stamp bales of grain and other property. Many of them have animal designs and show the great variety of wild animals known to the Indus Valley people: elephants, tigers, rhinoceroses, antelopes, crocodiles, and humped bulls.

◄ This is a drawing of a **terra-cotta** statuette of a mother-goddess figure found at Mohenjo-Daro. She is wearing a loincloth and jewelry.

Ancient India
*c.*2500 B.C.: Indus Valley civilization begins to emerge.
*c.*1500 B.C.: collapse of Indus Valley civilization.
*c.*1500 B.C.: Aryans settle in northern India and possibly destroy Indus Valley civilization.
*c.*800 B.C.: Aryan settlement expands southward.
*c.*563 B.C.: birth of the Buddha.
323 B.C.: Alexander the Great dies.
*c.*320 B.C.: Mauryan Empire founded in northern India.

Civilizations of Europe and the Mediterranean

The civilizations that succeeded those of Mesopotamia and Egypt grew up around the shores of the Mediterranean Sea.

The Israelites

The Israelites were a **Semitic** people related to both the Babylonians and the Assyrians. They migrated to Palestine in about 2000 B.C., and after a period of exile in Egypt, returned to Palestine. Here, under King David, they set up a kingdom with its capital at Jerusalem. Later, Palestine was split into two hostile kingdoms, Israel and Judah.

The Phoenicians

From 1200 B.C. the Phoenicians established themselves along the eastern shore of the Mediterranean, where they cultivated wheat, barley, olives, vines, and figs. Their main centers were the ports along the coast, such as Tyre and Sidon, from where they sailed all over the Mediterranean, trading goods — timber, glassware, metalwork, and ivory. In time they **colonized** much of the Mediterranean shore; the largest and most famous colony was Carthage.

One of the Phoenicians' most valued exports was the purple cloth that gives them their name (Phoenicia comes from

▲ Masada is a natural rock fortress near the Dead Sea. It was developed by Herod the Great, king of Judea, as a fort with storehouses, baths, a synagogue (place of worship), two palaces, and enough space in the center to grow some crops. In A.D. 72–73 a group of Jewish patriots called Zealots made a final stand at Masada against the Romans. Rather than surrender to the Roman troops, 960 Jews killed themselves.

The Hebrew kingdoms of Israel and Judah (later Judea) grew up in the region between the Jordan River and the Mediterranean Sea.

MEDITERRANEAN SEA

Sidon • PHOENICIA   Damascus •

Tyre •

ISRAEL
Samaria • • Tirzah
Shechem •   Jordan River
Jericho •
Jerusalem •
Bethlehem •
Gaza •   Hebron •   Dead Sea
PHILISTIA   JUDAH   MOAB
Beersheba • Masada •

0   50 miles
0   50 kilometers

continued on p. 32

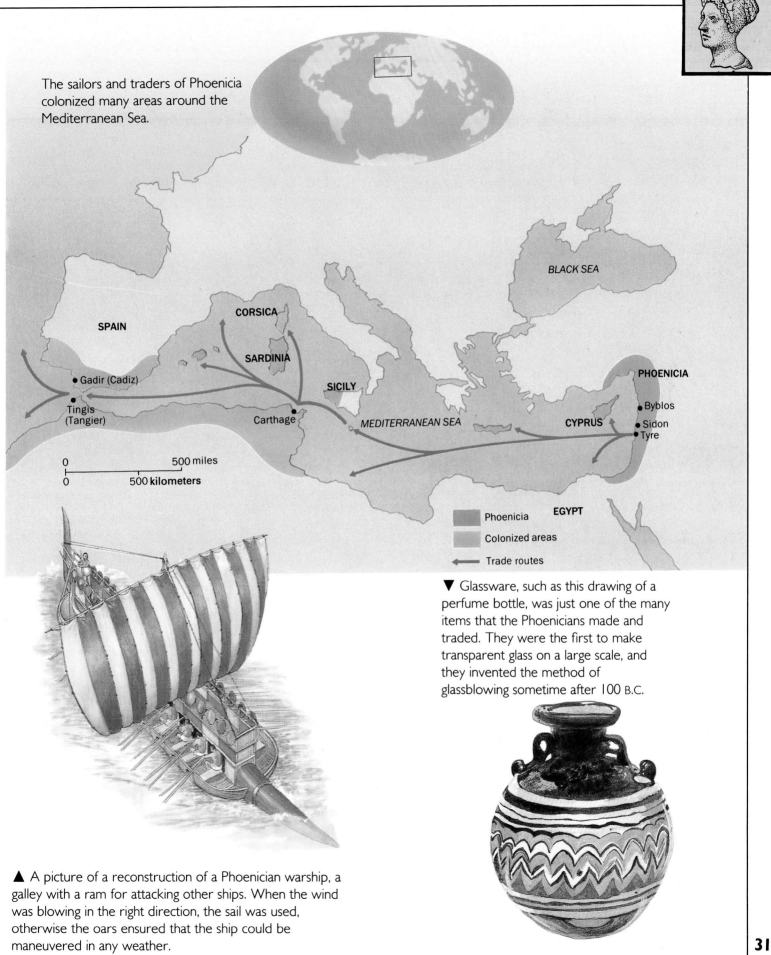

The sailors and traders of Phoenicia colonized many areas around the Mediterranean Sea.

BLACK SEA

SPAIN

CORSICA

SARDINIA

SICILY

PHOENICIA

● Gadir (Cadiz)

● Byblos

Tingis
(Tangier)

Carthage

MEDITERRANEAN SEA

CYPRUS

● Sidon

● Tyre

0   500 miles

0   500 kilometers

EGYPT

Phoenicia

Colonized areas

Trade routes

▼ Glassware, such as this drawing of a perfume bottle, was just one of the many items that the Phoenicians made and traded. They were the first to make transparent glass on a large scale, and they invented the method of glassblowing sometime after 100 B.C.

▲ A picture of a reconstruction of a Phoenician warship, a galley with a ram for attacking other ships. When the wind was blowing in the right direction, the sail was used, otherwise the oars ensured that the ship could be maneuvered in any weather.

the Greek word *phoinos*, meaning purple). The dye for the cloth was made from a substance produced from shellfish. The vivid purple color of the cloth became a symbol of authority in the Roman Empire.

Minos and Mycenae

The first European civilization—the Minoan civilization—was established on the island of Crete after about 2000 B.C. It was named after its legendary king, Minos. The Minoans built several large cities which were connected by a network of roads. Each of these cities centered around a palace; the largest and grandest was at Knossos, where there were royal apartments for the king and queen, rooms for religious rites, workshops for the skilled Minoan craftspeople, and a "schoolroom" where students learned to read and write in order to become scribes.

The Minoan civilization began to decline after about 1450 B.C., and the culture disappeared in the mid-1100's B.C. Whether it was destroyed by an earthquake or taken over by the Mycenaean Greeks is not certain.

The Mycenaean Greeks established a civilization in southeast Greece during the time of the Minoans and were at first influenced by them. However, the Mycenaeans were more warlike; their cities were built like fortresses, and they accumulated wealth not only by trade but also by plundering and raiding. They traded around the

continued on p. 34

▼ A death mask of beaten gold from a tomb at Mycenae. When it was first found, it was described as the mask of the legendary king Agamemnon. The Mycenaeans buried their kings and nobles in shaft graves, sunk vertically into solid rock. Beside the bodies they laid objects of bronze, gold, ivory, pottery, and silver. Later tombs were made by tunneling into hillsides.

▼ A room in the palace at Knossos showing some of the frescoes which cover the walls of the palace.

▼ The ruins of the Parthenon in Athens. The Parthenon was built between 447 and 438 B.C., and it was designed to impress by its size and splendor. Inside, the temple housed a finely worked statue in gold and ivory of Athena, the patron goddess of the city. There was an altar outside at which people worshiped and where sacrifices were possibly made.

▲ This little bronze statue of a girl athlete from Sparta is part of a lid of a vase found in Yugoslavia. Athenian girls were kept at home and taught how to be good housewives, however, girls from the city-state of Sparta were encouraged to lead much freer lives.

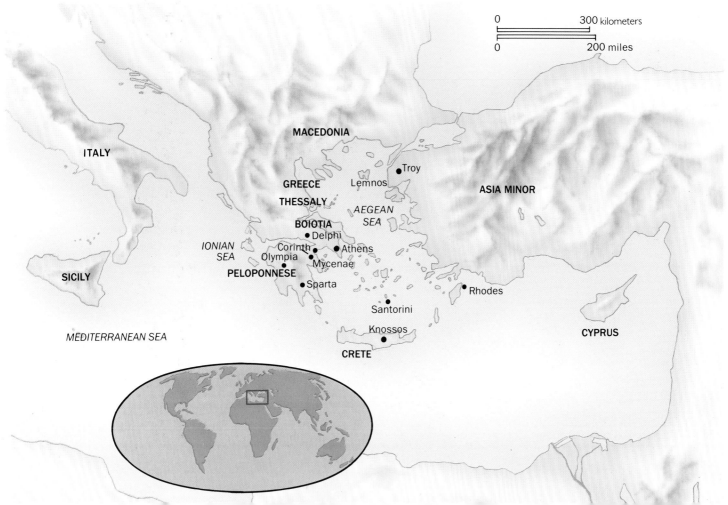

0   300 kilometers

0   200 miles

MACEDONIA

ITALY

Troy

GREECE   Lemnos

THESSALY   ASIA MINOR

AEGEAN
SEA

BOIOTIA
● Delphi

IONIAN   Corinth
SEA   Olympia   ● Athens
● Mycenae
SICILY   Rhodes
PELOPONNESE
● Sparta

Santorini

MEDITERRANEAN SEA   Knossos   CYPRUS

CRETE

Mediterranean, importing precious stones and metals, as well as copper and tin to make bronze. In exchange, they exported bronze weapons, jewelry, olive oil, wine, and wool.

Athenians and Spartans

The prominence of the Mycenaeans diminished after about 1100 B.C. In the mountainous Greek countryside, city-states gradually grew up on the small plains between the mountains. Communication was often difficult between the city-states, so each small state developed separately and had its own government and laws and often its own army, currency, and weights and measures. Each city-state was governed by an **aristocratic** family. Around the polis, or central city, of each state were the villages and farms of the ordinary people, where they grew wheat, olives, and vegetables and reared goats for cheese and milk.

Two of these city-states grew in importance: Sparta and Athens. The Athenians developed the idea of **democracy**, by which they meant that the people took a direct part in government. But "the people" included only the Athenian male **citizens**—women, slaves, and people who were not Athenians had no political rights.

In 480 B.C. Sparta and Athens united to fight a war against a common enemy — Persian invaders. But later in the same century (431–404 B.C.) they fought each other in a war that ruined Athens.

2000 B.C.–A.D. 456

▲ The picture on this amphora, or vase, shows a racing chariot with four horses at the Olympic Games. The games were originally held as a religious ceremony in honor of Zeus. Women held their own games in honor of the goddess Hera. The Olympic Games were held every four years from 776 B.C. to A.D. 394. In 520 B.C. the timetable for the events was as follows:

Day 1: sacrifices, oaths, checking of athletes.
Day 2: equestrian events, pentathlon.
Day 3: religious observations, boys' events.
Day 4: track events, wrestling, boxing, race in armor.
Day 5: banquet, sacrifices.

◀ While marble statues often portrayed heroic figures of gods and goddesses, little clay figures portrayed the everyday life of ordinary people. This figure was made in 500 B.C. and shows a woman grinding grain to make bread. Bread was the staple diet in most Greek towns, but eggs, vegetables, olives, grapes, and figs were also grown and eaten. Meat was usually only eaten after a sacrifice.

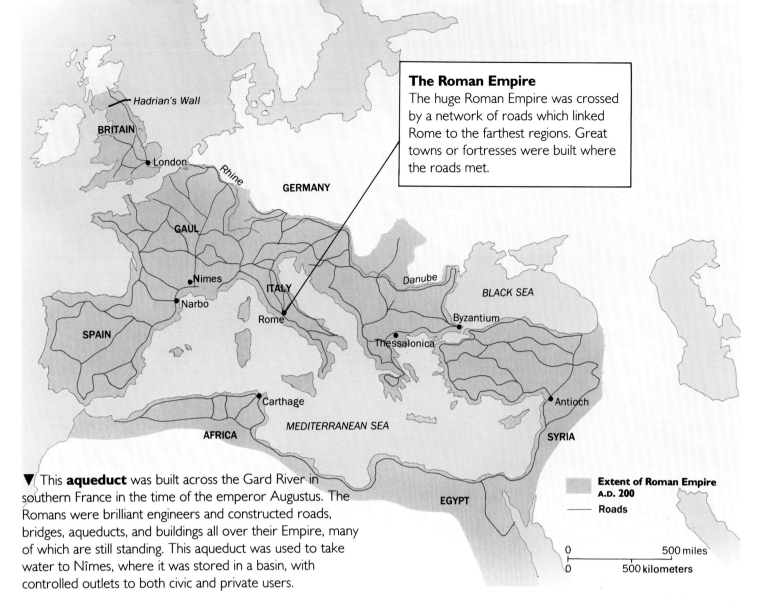

The Roman Empire
The huge Roman Empire was crossed by a network of roads which linked Rome to the farthest regions. Great towns or fortresses were built where the roads met.

Hadrian's Wall
BRITAIN
London
Rhine
GERMANY
GAUL
Nimes
Narbo
ITALY
Danube
BLACK SEA
Rome
Byzantium
Thessalonica
SPAIN
Antioch
Carthage
MEDITERRANEAN SEA
SYRIA
AFRICA
EGYPT

Extent of Roman Empire A.D. 200
Roads

0   500 miles
0   500 kilometers

▼ This **aqueduct** was built across the Gard River in southern France in the time of the emperor Augustus. The Romans were brilliant engineers and constructed roads, bridges, aqueducts, and buildings all over their Empire, many of which are still standing. This aqueduct was used to take water to Nîmes, where it was stored in a basin, with controlled outlets to both civic and private users.

► The ruins of the Colosseum, a huge **amphitheater** in the center of Rome. It was officially opened in A.D. 80 and could hold 50,000 spectators. Both men and women came to watch the bloody fights to the death between gladiators (usually prisoners of war or condemned criminals) or between wild beasts. Beneath the floor of the amphitheater were underground cages for the animals and a water system to flood the area for mock sea battles.

35

The Romans

The first civilization in Italy was that of the Etruscans, who established small independent city-states in the area that is now called Tuscany. We know little about the Etruscans, but they undoubtedly influenced their southern neighbors, the Romans, passing on, for example, their skill in building roads.

Rome itself was originally an Etruscan city, but in 509 B.C. the local "patricians," or aristocrats, overthrew the Etruscan king and set up a **republic**. At first the patricians governed Rome: they elected two **consuls** from among themselves who were advised by the **senate**. But gradually the "plebeians," or ordinary people, became more powerful and demanded a part in the government of Rome. After 367 B.C. it became the custom for one consul to be a plebeian.

By 44 B.C. the Romans ruled the whole Mediterranean world, either directly or by influence over native rulers. They linked together their huge Empire with a network of roads and controlled it with a well-disciplined army. Trade flourished as the Roman way of life became established in many parts of the Empire: wine, olive oil, wool, linen, silk, spices, fine pottery, and glass were all traded within the Empire.

The Roman Republic ended in a **civil war** in which one man, Octavian, gained supreme power. He was given the title Augustus and made himself emperor.

▲ Part of Trajan's Column, a monument built in Emperor Trajan's honor, which tells the story of two of the wars fought by the Roman army under Trajan's command. The soldiers were well trained and not only fought battles but also built bridges and fortresses. Here they are building a camp—some soldiers are digging a double ditch, while others construct ramparts out of pieces of turf.

▶ A relief sculpture of a Roman family at dinner. The men recline on a couch to eat. Slaves stand by to wait on them.

▼ In this relief sculpture a Roman butcher wields a cleaver similar to those used today. His wife sits in a chair doing the accounts.

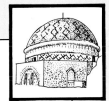

Religions of the Mediterranean Lands

Three important modern religions began close to the Mediterranean Sea: Judaism, Christianity, and Islam. Unlike the Eastern religions (*see page 27*), all three are based on a belief in one God.

Judaism

Judaism is the religion of Israel, and has been the religion of the Jews all over the world for more than 3,000 years. Jews believe in one God, who is the creator of all things.

The basis of Judaism is the Ten Commandments, which, according to tradition, God gave to the Jewish leader Moses sometime in the 1200s B.C. The commandments and laws based on them rule every aspect of Jewish life. The history and laws of the Jews are contained in the Old Testament of the Bible.

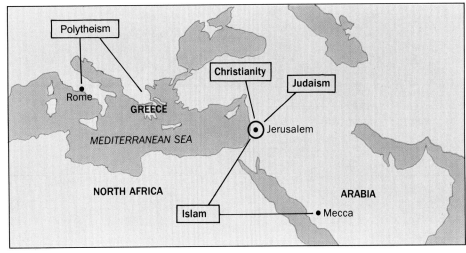

▲ A mosaic of the seven-branched candlestick, or menorah. A golden menorah stood in the tabernacle, the Jews' first holy temple.

Christianity

For centuries the Jews have believed that a Messiah (savior) would be born to lead them. At the time that Jesus of Nazareth was born, around 4 B.C., the Jews were under Roman rule. Jesus' followers believed him to be the promised Messiah, the son of God, but other Jews accused him of blasphemy, and he was tried before the Roman governor of Judea, Pontius Pilate. Jesus was crucified, probably in about A.D. 30, but his followers (disciples) reported having seen and talked to Jesus after his death. This resurrection formed the basis of the new religion that arose from the old traditions of Judaism: Christianity.

The life and teachings of Jesus are contained in the four Gospels of the New Testament of the Bible.

Islam

Islam is a much younger religion than either Judaism or Christianity. It was founded in the A.D. 600s by the prophet Muhammad. Muhammad was born in Mecca, an important trading center in Arabia. At that time most Arabs believed in nature gods,

▼ The Dome of the Rock, a Muslim mosque in Jerusalem. Jerusalem is a holy center for Jews, Christians, and Muslims.

spirits, and demons. One day, Muhammad was sitting outside a cave when he heard a voice telling him to set down the words of God. His writings over the next 22 years were put together to form the Koran—the holy book of Islam.

The followers of Islam are called Muslims, which means "those who submit." Muslims worship one god, Allah, and they have strict religious observances, including regular prayer.

Peoples of the West and South

Although the civilizations of Europe and eastern Asia lay far apart, they were linked by traders, even in ancient times. But there were two regions of the world that were completely cut off from the rest: the Americas and the Pacific. A third, Africa south of the Sahara, had comparatively few links.

The Americas

The first people to reach America probably walked across a land bridge where the Bering Strait now is (*see page 11*). The early Americans were hunters, fishers, and food gatherers. They used stone tools, and although metals such as gold, silver, and copper were worked with hammers, the secret of **smelting** was never discovered. Iron was not introduced into America until the European invasion in the A.D. 1500s.

Farming began in an area that archaeologists call **Mesoamerica**, which includes Central America and Mexico. Small villages grew up, and people grew maize (corn), beans, and pumpkins. Some of the earliest civilizations were also in this area: the Olmec culture with its center at La Venta, the Teotihuacán culture, and the beginnings of the Maya culture, which lasted until about A.D. 1000.

► This little pottery figure of a crying baby is the work of the Olmec Amerindians, who settled in communities on the coast of the Gulf of Mexico in around 500 B.C. Their center was at La Venta. They invented a type of hieroglyphic writing and a numerical system.

▼ Huge stone heads, some of them 9 feet tall and weighing 15 tons, were carved by the Olmecs. They are thought to represent gods. The Olmec sculptors also carved small figures out of jade and similar hard stone.

38

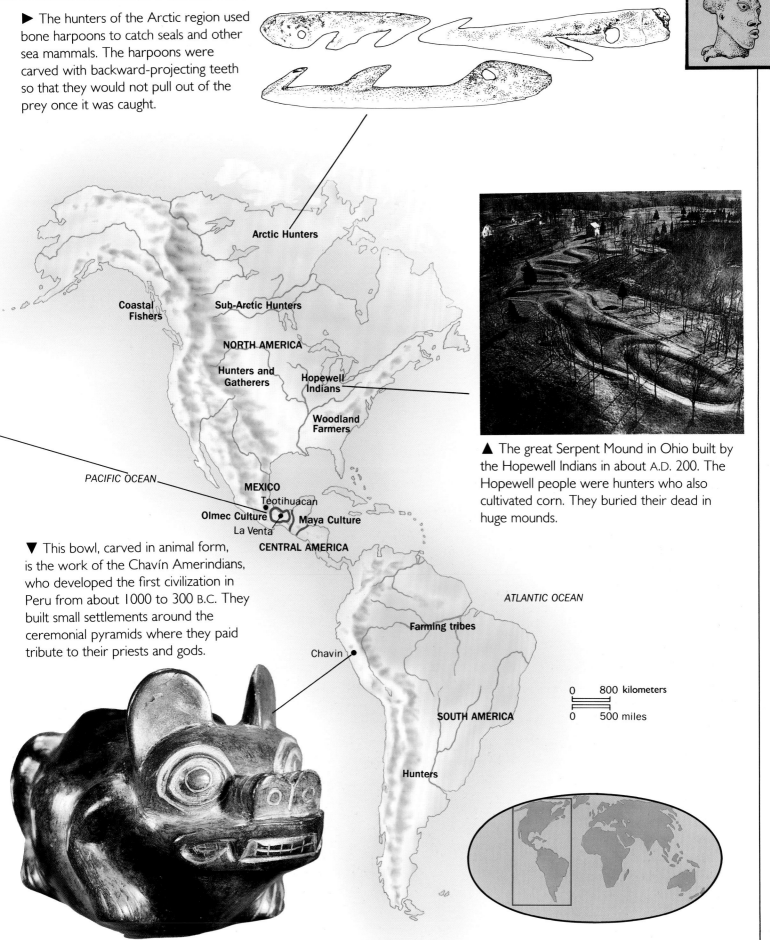

► The hunters of the Arctic region used bone harpoons to catch seals and other sea mammals. The harpoons were carved with backward-projecting teeth so that they would not pull out of the prey once it was caught.

Arctic Hunters

Coastal Fishers

Sub-Arctic Hunters

NORTH AMERICA

Hunters and Gatherers

Hopewell Indians

Woodland Farmers

PACIFIC OCEAN

MEXICO
Teotihuacan
Olmec Culture
La Venta
Maya Culture
CENTRAL AMERICA

▲ The great Serpent Mound in Ohio built by the Hopewell Indians in about A.D. 200. The Hopewell people were hunters who also cultivated corn. They buried their dead in huge mounds.

▼ This bowl, carved in animal form, is the work of the Chavín Amerindians, who developed the first civilization in Peru from about 1000 to 300 B.C. They built small settlements around the ceremonial pyramids where they paid tribute to their priests and gods.

ATLANTIC OCEAN

Farming tribes

Chavin

0   800 kilometers
0   500 miles

SOUTH AMERICA

Hunters

39

African empires

Up until the end of the last ice age the area that we now call the Sahara was not desert but wet grassland. In this fertile region the early African peoples cultivated wheat and barley and herded cattle. But after about 2500 B.C. the climate slowly became warmer, and the Sahara began to dry out. Some of the farmers moved gradually southward to the **tropical** regions of the interior. Here, after about 2000 B.C., sorghum, millet, and yams were cultivated; elsewhere, in places where the jungle was too thick for crop growing, local economies sometimes depended on fishing.

The earliest African civilization south of the great Egyptian Empire (*see pages 16–18*) was the kingdom of Kush, which flourished on the banks of the Nile from about 500 B.C. to A.D. 350. Its capital, Meroë, was an important center for ironworking from about 500 B.C., and this skill quickly spread south. People could now make iron tools and weapons; cultivation was easier and crop yields improved.

The Bantu peoples

South of the rainforests of the Congo Basin, the earliest inhabitants were hunters: the San and the Khoikhoi peoples. But gradually a new group of people migrated from their homeland in the north and west and developed their own cultures. They had one common feature–their languages all came from **Bantu**.

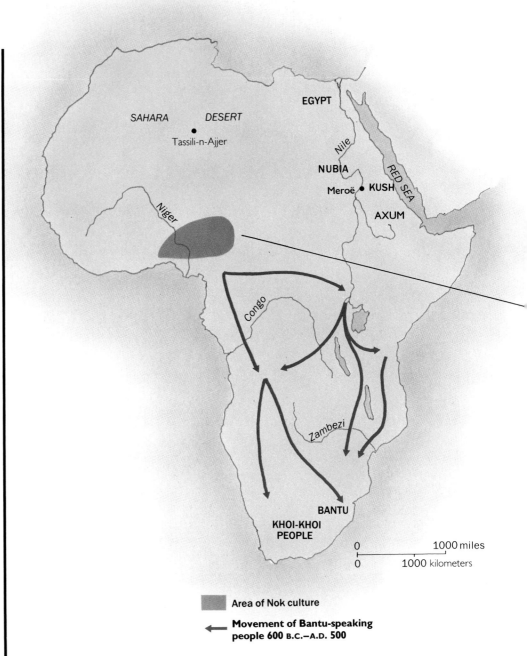

Area of Nok culture

Movement of Bantu-speaking people 600 B.C.–A.D. 500

▼ Methods of iron smelting were developed in Africa after about 500 B.C. In this picture the furnace is built of compacted earth, and bellows (to blow air) are used to reach the high temperatures necessary to turn the iron ore into metal. The metal produced was used to make strong tools and weapons.

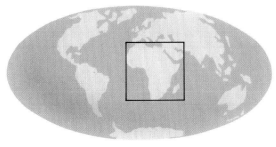

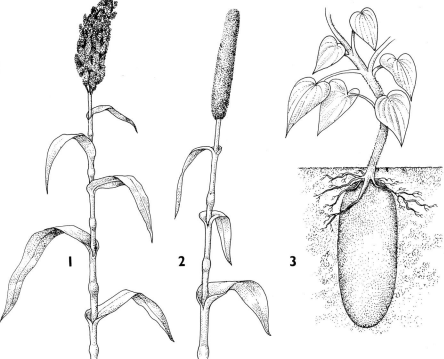

▼ One of the fine terra-cotta heads found near the village of Nok, in northern Nigeria. This type of sculpture flourished in the area from about 400 B.C. to A.D. 200.

▲ Three important crops which were cultivated by early farmers south of the Sahara.
1. Sorghum, an important early crop.
2. Millet, faster growing than sorghum and able to withstand a drier climate.
3. Yam, a nutritious tuber.

▼ Rock paintings and relief carvings are found all over Africa. This lively cattle-herding scene comes from the Tassili-n-Ajjer Mountains in the Sahara. The first **pastoralists** in the Sahara region domesticated goats and sheep; later many different breeds of cattle were kept.

Australia and Oceania

The first people migrated to Australia between 70,000 and 50,000 years ago. At that time the sea levels were lower than they are today, so Australia, New Guinea, and Tasmania were all linked by huge land bridges, forming a land mass called Greater Australia. The first Australians, ancestors of the Aborigines, had to sail across the sea from Southeast Asia to reach the nearest point of Greater Australia.

Around 6,000 years ago the sea rose to its present level, and the Aboriginal people began to move into the interior and exploit the natural resources found there. The Aborigines were fishers, hunters, and gatherers: they never developed a system of agriculture or cattle rearing. They developed their own culture until the arrival of the Europeans in the A.D. 1700s.

The smaller Pacific Islands that make up Oceania—spread out over the vast Pacific Ocean—were colonized much later. The first people sailed from the Moluccas region of Indonesia in about 2000 B.C. These people were able to build large canoes that could survive long voyages and transport not only themselves but also their supplies, animals, and some of the plants they grew. They sailed first to the islands of Melanesia. Then in about 1300 B.C. they reached Fiji, Samoa, and Tonga. The farthest islands of Oceania, and New Zealand, were not settled until at least A.D. 800.

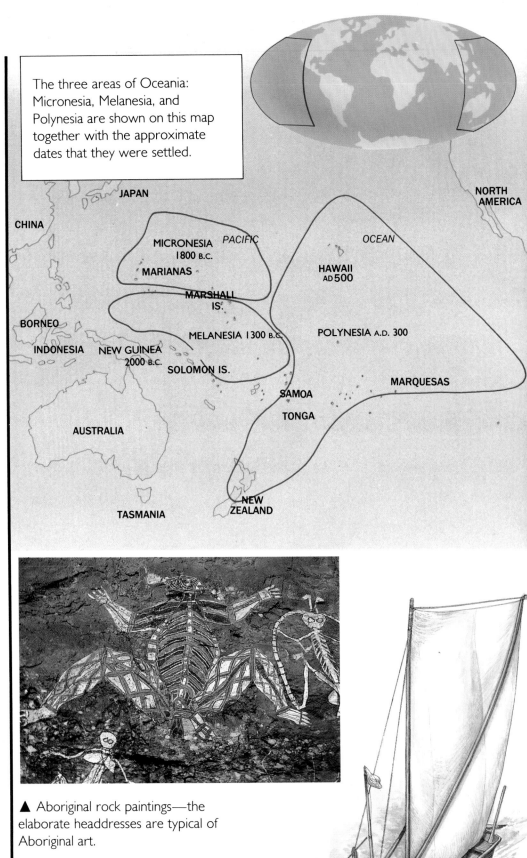

The three areas of Oceania: Micronesia, Melanesia, and Polynesia are shown on this map together with the approximate dates that they were settled.

▲ Aboriginal rock paintings—the elaborate headdresses are typical of Aboriginal art.

▶ A canoe from southeast Papua New Guinea, similar to those used by the early peoples in Oceania.

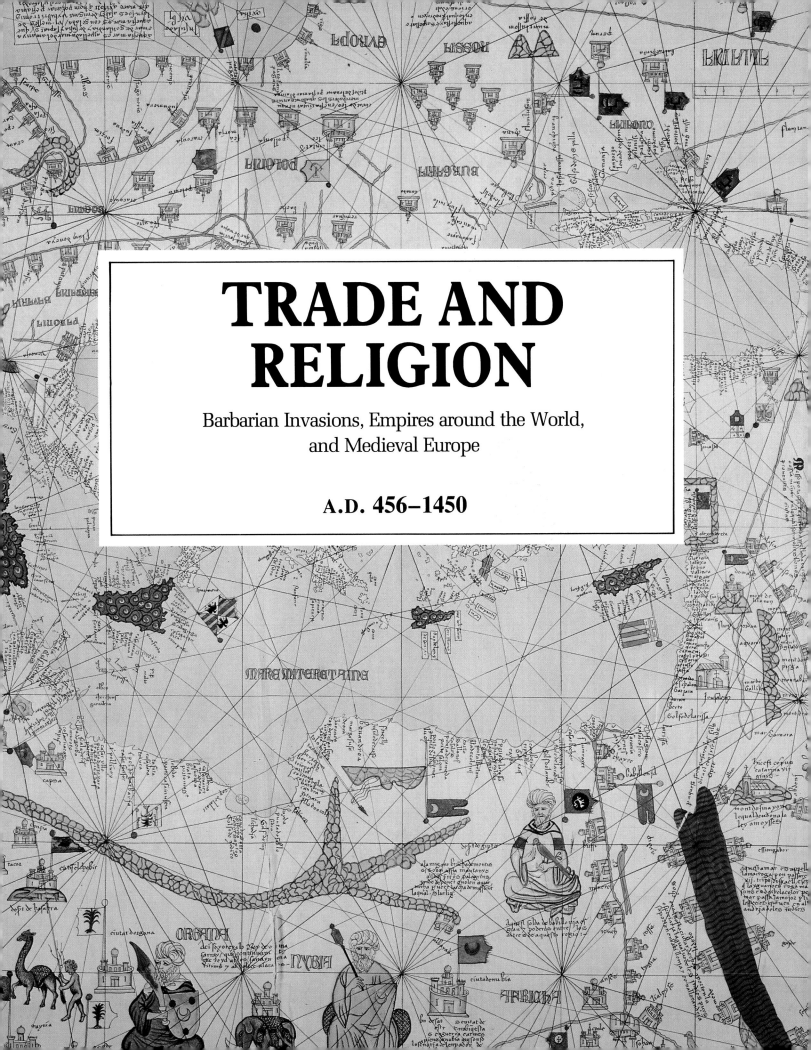

TRADE AND RELIGION

Barbarian Invasions, Empires around the World,
and Medieval Europe

A.D. 456–1450

The World in 450 and After

The world in A.D. 450

About 2,000 years ago, most people in the world lived within four great empires. The Roman Empire was the most powerful, and controlled Europe and northern Africa. To the east, the Han dynasty (family) governed much of what is now modern China. Between them lay the rich Sassanian Empire in the Middle East and the great Gupta Empire of India.

These powerful empires were secure and fairly peaceful, with strong governments and wealthy **economies**. Trade linked them all together. Land travel was slow, however, and many goods were transported on boats, which crossed both the Indian Ocean and the Mediterranean Sea. These trading contacts brought the peoples of the four empires together and helped the spread of religious and other ideas.

These links did not stretch across either the Pacific or Atlantic oceans. As a result, the peoples of Australia and America developed cultures of their own. Much of Africa, too, developed independently of the rest of the world.

By A.D. 450 the great empires of the world were under threat from various warlike **tribes** of nomads in northern Europe and parts of Asia. Within a few years these tribes would disrupt the settled empires.

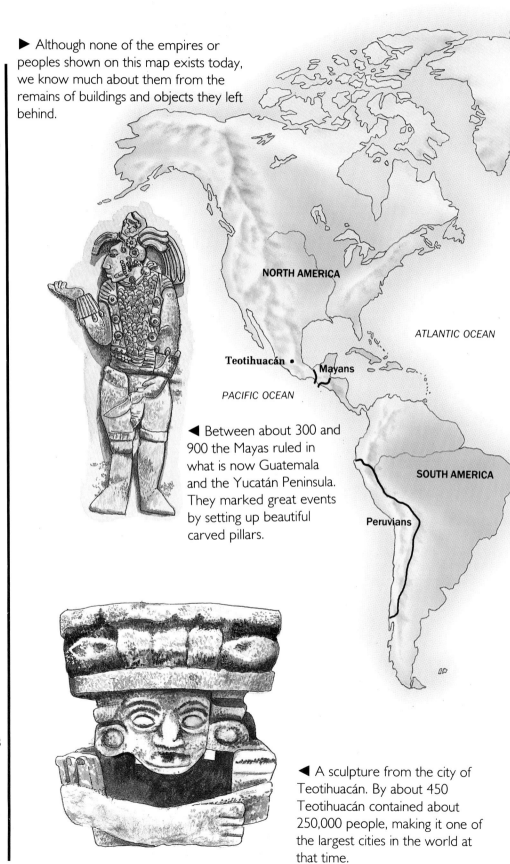

▶ Although none of the empires or peoples shown on this map exists today, we know much about them from the remains of buildings and objects they left behind.

◀ Between about 300 and 900 the Mayas ruled in what is now Guatemala and the Yucatán Peninsula. They marked great events by setting up beautiful carved pillars.

◀ A sculpture from the city of Teotihuacán. By about 450 Teotihuacán contained about 250,000 people, making it one of the largest cities in the world at that time.

44

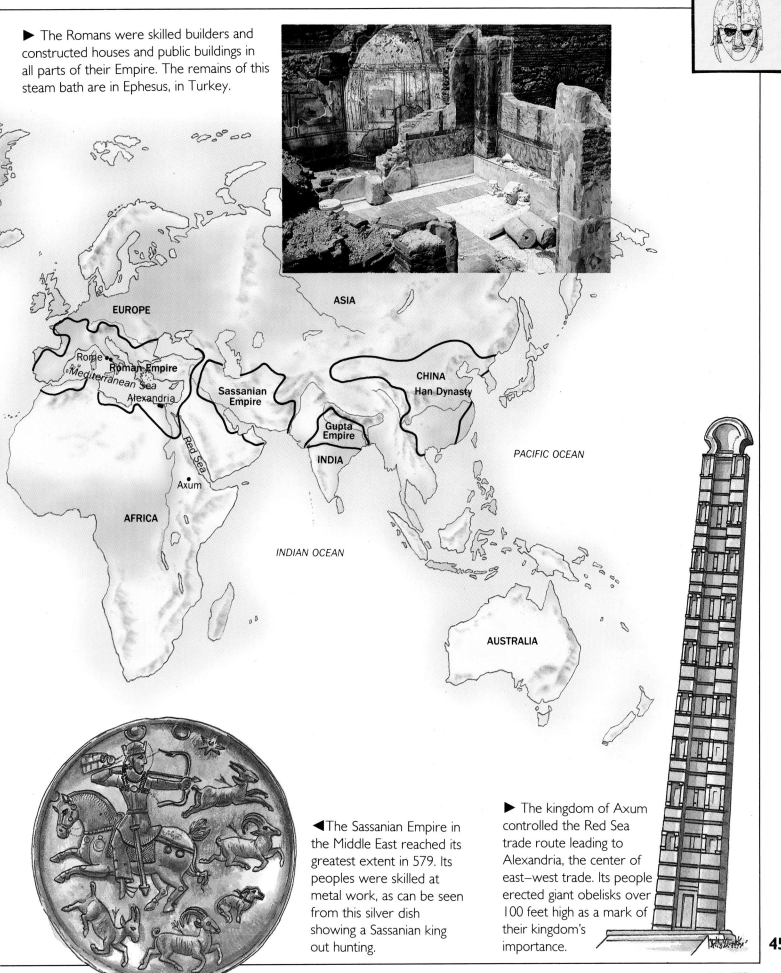

► The Romans were skilled builders and constructed houses and public buildings in all parts of their Empire. The remains of this steam bath are in Ephesus, in Turkey.

EUROPE

ASIA

Rome
Roman Empire
Mediterranean Sea
Alexandria

Sassanian Empire

CHINA
Han Dynasty

Gupta Empire

INDIA

Red Sea

Axum

AFRICA

PACIFIC OCEAN

INDIAN OCEAN

AUSTRALIA

◄The Sassanian Empire in the Middle East reached its greatest extent in 579. Its peoples were skilled at metal work, as can be seen from this silver dish showing a Sassanian king out hunting.

► The kingdom of Axum controlled the Red Sea trade route leading to Alexandria, the center of east–west trade. Its people erected giant obelisks over 100 feet high as a mark of their kingdom's importance.

The collapse of empires

Ever since 200 B.C. the four empires in Europe and Asia had come under threat from heavily armed nomadic tribes. The Romans called them **barbarians**, for they were not educated and were not Christians. Nor did they live in settled towns but in tents on the vast **steppes** of central Asia. They traveled thousands of miles in search of grazing land, and when the **pasture** land was exhausted, or if they were attacked by rival tribes, they moved in search of new land, threatening the settled empires to the south and west.

At first, both the Romans and Chinese kept the nomads out, building strong defenses such as Hadrian's Wall in Britain and the Great Wall in China. These defenses were expensive, and the high **taxes** imposed to pay for them caused rebellions which weakened both the Chinese and Roman empires.

China was the first empire to fall. In A.D. 220 the Hsiungnu peoples of central Asia attacked China and ended Han rule in the country. The Huns, part of the Hsiungnu tribe, killed the Persian emperor in 484, and by 535 had destroyed the Gupta Empire in India.

But it was the Roman Empire that suffered the most. Tribes had attacked the Roman Empire as early as 167, but after 370 the attacks were more serious and Rome was overrun. In 476 the last Roman emperor was overthrown and the Empire was replaced by small tribal kingdoms.

46

▲ Because little written evidence exists about the fall of the Roman Empire, we have to learn about it from craftworks, buildings, and carvings. This carving is on the side of a tomb dating from around A.D. 200 and shows Roman soldiers fighting German invaders.

▶ The peoples who invaded the Roman Empire were skilled craftworkers. This elaborate helmet of iron, bronze, and silver was made by the Saxon invaders of Britain in about 625.

▼ Many of the tribes that invaded the Roman Empire adopted its officia' religion of Christianity. This gold helmet plaque shows an Ostrogoth ruler surrounded by angels.

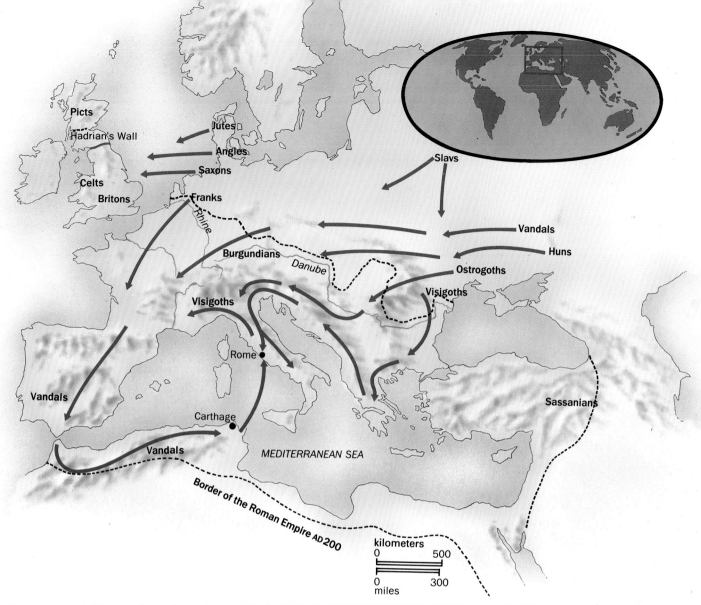

From about 167 a number of warring tribes attacked the long land frontier of the Roman Empire in central Europe. At first they were kept out of the Empire. But when the Huns arrived in eastern Europe from central Asia in around 370, many tribes started pouring over the frontier. The Visigoths sacked Rome in 410 and moved on to settle in southern Spain; the Vandals had moved into Spain by 409 and then northern Africa in 429. In the north, the Franks settled in what is now France, while the Angles, Saxons, and Jutes invaded Britain.

▶ The Vandals invaded northern Africa and set up their capital at Carthage. They took over the existing city and lived in the Roman houses, adopting Roman clothes and ways of life. This **mosaic**, made in about 500, shows a Vandal warrior leaving his villa as if he were a Roman citizen, not a conqueror.

47

The Byzantine Empire

In 284 Diocletian became Roman emperor. He decided that the huge Empire could only be ruled effectively by splitting it into two parts, east and west. In 330 his successor, Constantine, rebuilt the old Greek port of Byzantium, at the entrance to the Black Sea. He renamed it Constantinople. This city became the capital of the eastern half of the Empire. When the western half collapsed during the next century, Constantinople became the capital of the new Byzantine Empire.

At first, this Empire controlled only a small area around the eastern Mediterranean, but during the reign of Justinian (527–565), it started to recover much of the territory of the old Roman Empire. North Africa, Italy, and southern Spain were all reconquered.

The Byzantine Empire was wealthy and produced gold, silk, grain, olives, and wine. It traded these for spices, precious stones, and ivory from countries as far away as China and India. The Empire was a center of learning, combining the knowledge of the Greeks with the teachings of the Christian Church.

However, by 750 the last invaders from the east — Bulgars, Slavs, and Lombards — reduced the Empire to the small area that is now Greece and Turkey, and it never regained its strength. Yet it lasted until 1453, when the city of Constantinople was finally captured by the Turks.

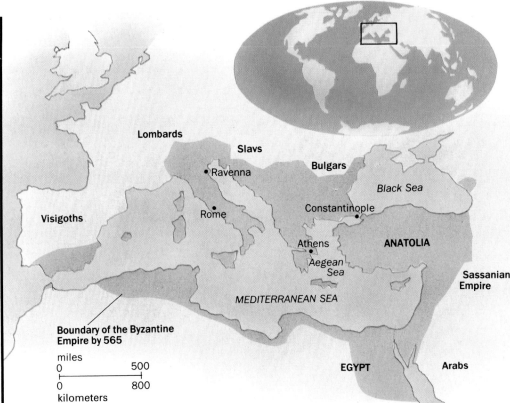

▲ The Byzantine Empire was ruled from its capital city of Constantinople, known today as Istanbul. At first the Empire lay around the Aegean Sea. It reached its greatest extent under Justinian, when it spread across the Mediterranean to Spain. However, it was always under threat from its warlike neighbors.

▼ This old map of Constantinople shows fortifications and many fine buildings. The city was an important trading center and commanded both the sea route between the Mediterranean and the Black Sea, and the land route between Europe and Asia and on to China.

48

▼ Many churches and public buildings in the Byzantine Empire were decorated with elaborate mosaics. These were made of thousands of colored glass cubes set in plaster. Some of the cubes were covered with gold or silver dust to make them glisten in the light.

▼ The Byzantine Empire was often under attack both from sea and from land. The secret weapon of the Byzantine navy was "Greek fire," a chemical mixture which burst into flames when it touched water.

▲ Under Justinian and Empress Theodora, the Byzantine Empire was a center for the arts and learning. This mosaic of Justinian is in the Church of San Vitale in Ravenna, for a time the capital of the Byzantine Empire in Italy.

The decimal system
Sometime after A.D. 400 the Guptas of India developed a new method of counting, which was based on multiples of 10. They used the symbol 0 to represent zero and the symbol . to separate whole numbers from fractions. From this came the decimal system that we use today. The Guptas also designed a simple way of writing numbers. We call these numbers Arabic numerals because like the decimal system, they came to us from the Arabs, whose traders learned them in India and brought them to Europe sometime after 1300.

The Religious World

All of the major religions began in Asia. Three of them — Judaism, Christianity, and **Islam** — started in the Middle East, and their followers regard Jerusalem as a holy city. These religions spread across the world as **missionaries**, traders, and other people traveled along the trade routes.

Early Christianity

Christianity began in the Roman province of Judea, in what is now Israel. Originally it was part of the Jewish religion. But in about A.D. 30 when its founder, Jesus Christ, was put to death by the Romans, his followers became known as Christians and founded a new religion based on the teachings of Christ.

The early Christians traveled throughout the Roman Empire preaching the message of Christ. At first, the Romans persecuted them. But in 312 the Roman emperor Constantine legalized Christianity, and it became the official religion of the Roman Empire in 392. Christianity grew in strength because it offered hope to its followers in the troubled times. Many of the invading tribes also adopted Christianity, but it spread slowly, and in some places, such as the British Isles, the early Christians had to struggle to keep the religion alive.

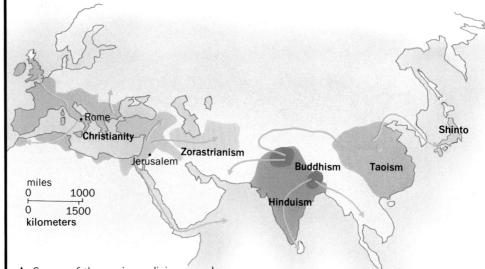

▲ Some of the major religions, such as Christianity and Buddhism, have spread from Asia throughout the world. Others, such as Hinduism and Taoism, have not spread beyond their country of origin.

Christianity spread from the Middle East, west throughout the Roman Empire, south into Egypt and Ethiopia, and east into Persia (Iran). It may also have reached India. Missionaries set up Christian communities in places such as the island of Iona off the west coast of Scotland. This cross (*right*) was built on Iona by early Christian missionaries. They also built churches decorated with the likeness of Jesus (*below*).

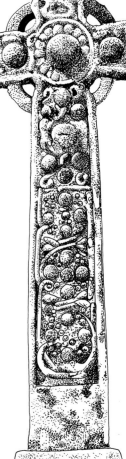

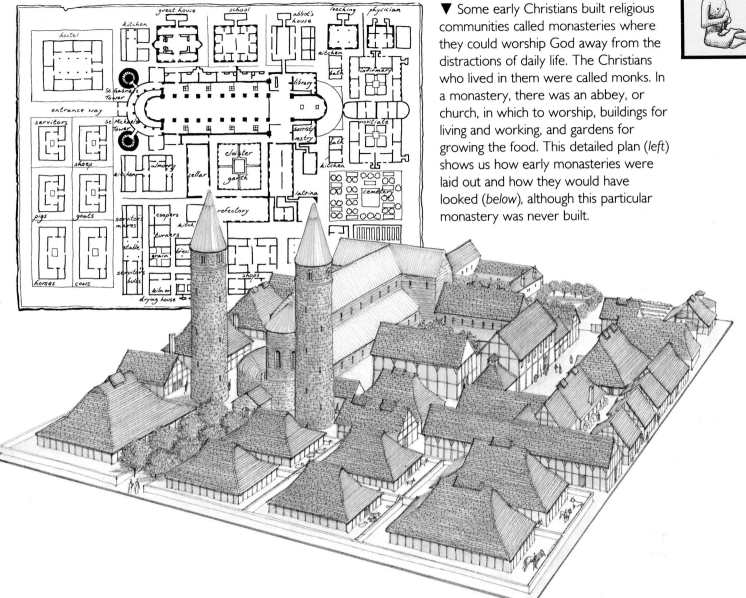

The plan labels (from the monastery plan, left) include:

hostel · kitchen · guest house · school · abbot's house · teaching · physician · St Gabriel's Tower · library · kitchen · bath · infirmary · entrance way · servitors · St Michael's Tower · novitiate · sheep · almonry · cloister · garth · sacristy · vestry · bath · kitchen · pigs · goats · cellar · kitchen · latrina · cemetery · servitors mares · coopers · kitch · turners · refectory · stable · grain · brew · horses · cows · servitors beds · shops · kiln or drying house

▼ Some early Christians built religious communities called monasteries where they could worship God away from the distractions of daily life. The Christians who lived in them were called monks. In a monastery, there was an abbey, or church, in which to worship, buildings for living and working, and gardens for growing the food. This detailed plan (*left*) shows us how early monasteries were laid out and how they would have looked (*below*), although this particular monastery was never built.

▶ Monasteries were important centers of learning because monks were usually the only people who could read and write. Monks drew up official documents, kept records, and wrote letters. They also copied books (*right*), which was the only way a book could be reproduced, for printing presses were unknown in Europe until 1453. Copying was done by hand and could take many years. Some monks were skilled illustrators, as can be seen from this detail (*far right*) in the beautiful Book of Kells, a religious manuscript which was produced on the Scottish island of Iona in about 800.

The rise of Islam

In the 600s a new religion began in Arabia. It was called Islam, which means "submission to the will of Allah (God)." Within 100 years more than half the total population of Europe and Asia was Muslim (the name given to followers of Islam).

Islam was founded by a prophet named Muhammad. He came from the Arabian city of Mecca, and in about 610 began to develop the teachings of the Koran, the holy book of Islam. The new religion threatened the old gods worshiped in Mecca, so in 622 Muhammad and his followers were forced to flee to Medina.

From Medina, Muhammad and his followers organized the first Muslim **state** and built the first mosque. Although Arabia was a wealthy region, most of the population was very poor. Many of these poor people were attracted to Islam because its teachings offered them a fairer society.

In 630 Muhammad attacked and captured Mecca. Under his rule, Mecca became the capital of an Islamic empire that controlled most of the Arabian peninsula. After Muhammad's death in 632, Muslim armies spread the Islamic religion eastward to India and westward across northern Africa and into Spain. The Byzantine Empire was seriously weakened and lost all its lands in Africa. But the Muslims were defeated by the Franks in France at the battle of Poitiers in 732, and their empire extended no farther.

▲ The Kaaba in Mecca houses a sacred black stone and is the center of the Islamic world. At certain times during the day every observant Muslim in the world faces toward it to pray. **Pilgrims** to Mecca walk around it seven times in homage.

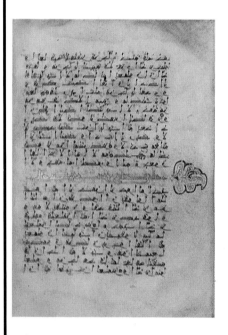

◀ The Koran is the holy book of Islam. Muslims believe that it is the word of God as told to His prophet Muhammad. The Koran contains religious beliefs as well as social and political instructions.

▼ Islam began in Arabia but quickly spread throughout the Middle East and northern Africa. Although united by one faith, the Islamic world soon broke up into separate countries.

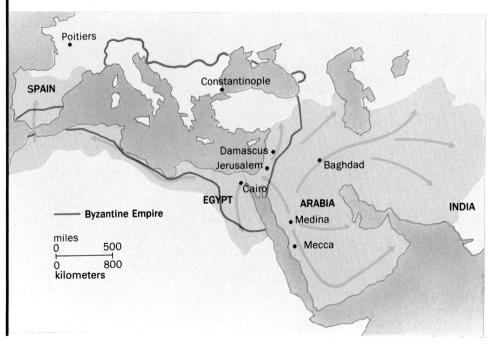

Poitiers

SPAIN

Constantinople

Damascus

Jerusalem

Baghdad

Cairo

EGYPT

ARABIA

INDIA

Medina

Mecca

——— Byzantine Empire

miles
0   500

0   800
kilometers

In 762 al-Mansur, the leader of the Islamic world, built a new capital city at Baghdad in what is now Iraq. He made it a center of learning and culture. There was an observatory to study the stars and a "House of Learning" in which scholars studied mathematics and translated the writings of the ancient Greeks into Arabic. Christian and Jewish scholars were welcomed because Islam was tolerant of other religions. Cairo, in Egypt, was also a center of learning, and in 971 the world's first university was opened there. The arts flourished throughout the Islamic world, particularly calligraphy and writing. This was because it was forbidden to draw or paint human figures in religious pictures.

▲ Arab astronomers, like the ancient Greeks, showed the constellations of the stars as human figures. The constellation shown here is Cepheus.

▲ Water was scarce in the hot, dry climate of the Islamic world. Arab engineers were skilled in methods of raising water from the ground and piping it into their homes.

▲ In 1154 Arab mapmakers drew this map of the world. It shows that they were familiar with the basic outlines of Asia, northern Africa, and Europe. But like the Europeans at this time, they did not know that Australia or America existed.

▲ Arab medicine was very advanced. Islamic pharmacists were skilled in making suitable drugs for treating illnesses.

The Buddhist world

Buddhism, one of the world's major religions, began as an offshoot of Hinduism, an Indian religion that dates back to 1500 B.C. and is still widely practiced today. The Hindus divide people up into social classes called **castes**. They believe that a person is born into one particular caste and can not leave it during his or her lifetime. But many people disliked this strict system because it meant that nothing could be changed and that suffering and poverty were allowed to continue.

In about 525 B.C. an Indian prince named Siddhartha Gautama, who had left his rich family to travel and study, began to preach another message. He said that it was possible to overcome suffering and reach a state of total peace, which he called "Nirvana."

By the time of his death in 483 B.C. Gautama had become known as the Buddha, or "the Enlightened One," and his teachings had spread throughout India. In about 257 B.C. the Indian ruler Asoka became a Buddhist, and Buddhism became a major force throughout southern Asia. Missionaries spread the religion north to Afghanistan, Tibet, China, and Japan. In Japan it became the official religion in A.D. 594. Missionaries also spread Buddhism south to Burma and the rest of Indochina. Buddhism gained strength from the upheavals caused by the nomadic invasions.

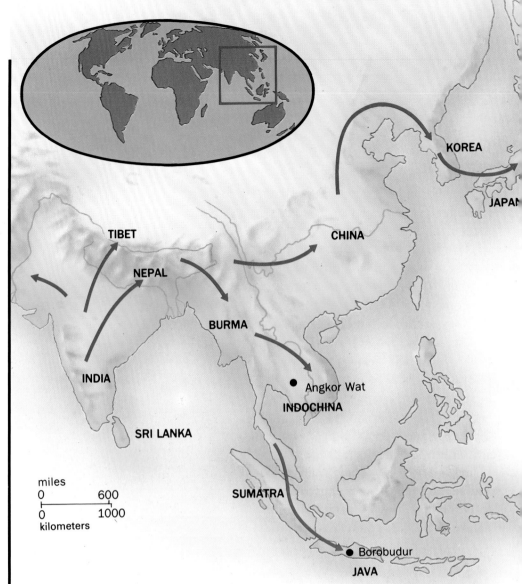

▲ Missionaries spread the Buddhist religion from India north to Afghanistan, Tibet, China, and Japan and south to Burma and Indochina, often following trade routes.

▼ The Buddhist temple of Borobudur in Java was built in about 800. It has ten levels. Each level represents the different stages of a person's life from ignorance to Nirvana, the ultimate Buddhist aim.

54

▶ When the Chinese princess Yung T'ai was only 17, she was forced to commit suicide for criticizing her grandmother, the Chinese empress Wu (690–713). Yung T'ai's tomb is decorated with portraits of court ladies accompanied by servants waiting on the princess.

▼ During the time of the Sui dynasty in China (581–618), more than 100,000 statues of Buddha were built, some out of solid rock, and nearly 4,000 temples were constructed.

Footbinding
In Chinese culture, small feet were considered a sign of beauty. The daughters of the wealthy classes had their feet bound tightly with silk when they were very young. As they grew up, their feet stayed so small that the women could not walk without considerable pain. Footbinding continued in China almost to the present day.

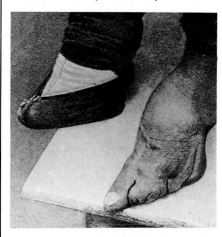

Empires and Invasions

Charlemagne and the Holy Roman Empire

Charlemagne, or Charles the Great, was the most famous ruler of the Middle Ages. Charlemagne was a Frank, one of the peoples who had invaded the Roman Empire and settled in what is now central France. Prior to Charlemagne's time, the leader of the Franks was Clovis I, a Christian who had founded the Merovingian dynasty of kings. But following Frankish tradition, Clovis divided his kingdom between his four sons. This division weakened the kingdom, and power fell into the hands of leading officials. In 751 one official, Pepin, overthrew the Merovingians and formed the Carolingian dynasty. In 768 Pepin's sons, Carloman and Charlemagne, inherited the kingdom. When his brother died in 771, Charlemagne took full control.

Charlemagne soon conquered the rest of France and extended his kingdom into what is now Germany, Italy, and the Netherlands. He forcibly converted the Saxons and Avars who lived in central Europe to Christianity. On Christmas Day in 800, the pope crowned Charlemagne emperor of the Romans. At Charlemagne's death in 814 the Franks were the most powerful force in western Europe.

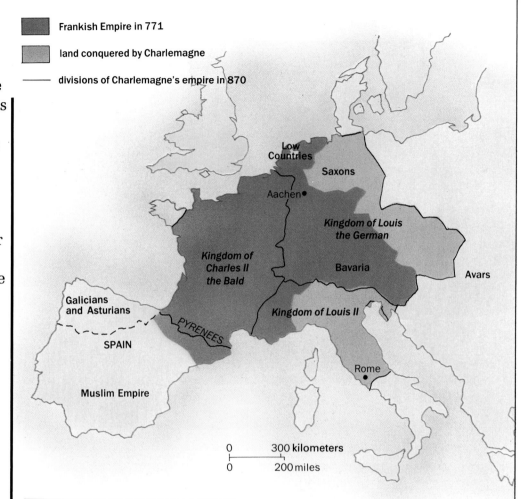

Legend:
- Frankish Empire in 771
- land conquered by Charlemagne
- divisions of Charlemagne's empire in 870

Low Countries · Saxons · Aachen · Kingdom of Louis the German · Kingdom of Charles II the Bald · Bavaria · Avars · Galicians and Asturians · Kingdom of Louis II · PYRENEES · SPAIN · Rome · Muslim Empire

0 300 kilometers
0 200 miles

The Holy Roman Empire

When Charlemagne was crowned in 800, he founded an empire that later became known as the Holy Roman Empire. This Empire lasted until 1806, when it ended because of French emperor Napoleon Bonaparte's rise to power. An empire was revived briefly between 1871 and 1918 when Germany was united as one country for the first time. Between 1933 and 1945, the German dictator, Adolf Hitler, attempted to build a Third Reich (empire) to last another 1,000 years, but he was defeated.

▲ Charlemagne's empire stretched from northern Spain across Europe to Germany and Italy. When it was divided between his three grandsons in 843, and again in 870, the boundaries of present-day France, Italy, and Germany became recognizable for the first time.

▼ The scholars who came to Charlemagne's court at Aachen in Germany developed a new style of handwriting in which to write their books. This Carolingian **minuscule** was used by the first printers 650 years later when they designed a type in which to print the first books.

B EATISSIMO PAPAE DAMASO bIERONIMUS

Trade and Transportation

Before cars, trains, and airplanes were invented, most people never left the town or village in which they were born. People worked within walking distance of their houses, and no one took vacations away from home. The only people who traveled were soldiers, traders, government officials, and pilgrims going to visit religious sites. They walked or rode on horseback along rough roads, and their journeys were slow and often dangerous. On land, robbers attacked foot travelers, and pirate raids were common at sea. Despite these problems, many travelers covered great distances, and the main roads were often very busy.

◄ Traveling could be hazardous. Here a traveler surrenders his money to a highwayman.

▲ Trade was carried across the Indian Ocean by ships called *dhows*. These simple but safe ships had lots of room for both passengers and cargo.

◄ Merchants, craftworkers, and buyers gathered at the fairs which were held in large towns all over Europe. This fair at Lendit in France started off as a religious festival.

▲ The **Silk Road** was the main land route between China and Europe. It was 2,500 miles long, and the best way to travel along it was by camel.

Viking invasions

Peace in western Europe did not last long. After 900, Muslim Arabs from northern Africa conquered Italy and crossed the Pyrenees to threaten France. The Magyars, a group of Asian nomads, raided Germany and Italy.

But the most powerful threat came from the Viking peoples of Scandinavia — Sweden, Norway, and Denmark. They left their homes in search of wealth and better farmland. They were skilled seafarers and sailed vast distances in their open longboats.

In 793 the Vikings raided Britain and soon occupied the northern half of the country. They established colonies in Ireland, and by 911 had settled in northern France, where they became known as Normans. They also traveled to Iceland and Greenland, and in 1003, reached Vinland (probably Newfoundland, Canada) almost 500 years before the Genoese explorer Columbus claimed to have discovered the same continent. A group of Vikings from Sweden, known as the Rus, set up trading posts at Novgorod and Kiev, giving their name — Russia — to the country they colonized.

Stories of the exploits of the Vikings were written by the people they attacked. These accounts naturally describe the Vikings as savage raiders, but they were also skilled craft-workers. The colonies they founded grew rich on trade, and the Vikings soon settled peacefully with the peoples they had once fought.

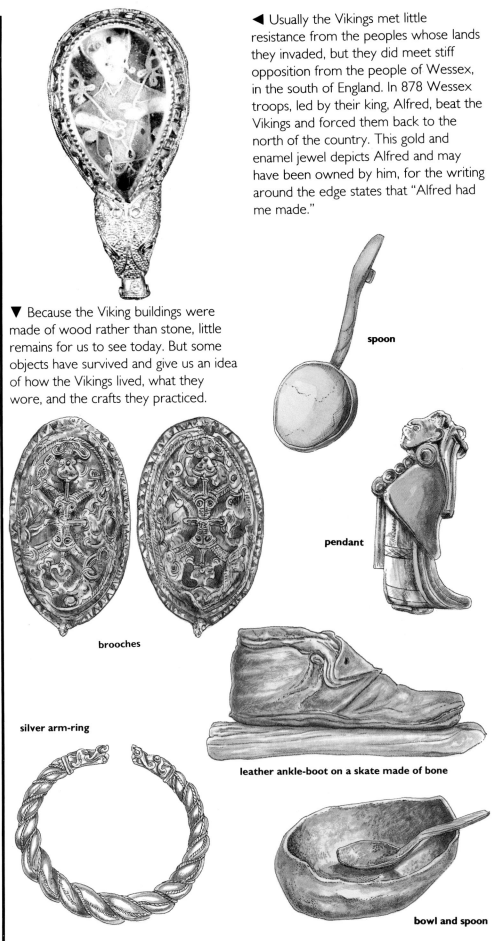

▼ Because the Viking buildings were made of wood rather than stone, little remains for us to see today. But some objects have survived and give us an idea of how the Vikings lived, what they wore, and the crafts they practiced.

◄ Usually the Vikings met little resistance from the peoples whose lands they invaded, but they did meet stiff opposition from the people of Wessex, in the south of England. In 878 Wessex troops, led by their king, Alfred, beat the Vikings and forced them back to the north of the country. This gold and enamel jewel depicts Alfred and may have been owned by him, for the writing around the edge states that "Alfred had me made."

spoon

pendant

brooches

silver arm-ring

leather ankle-boot on a skate made of bone

bowl and spoon

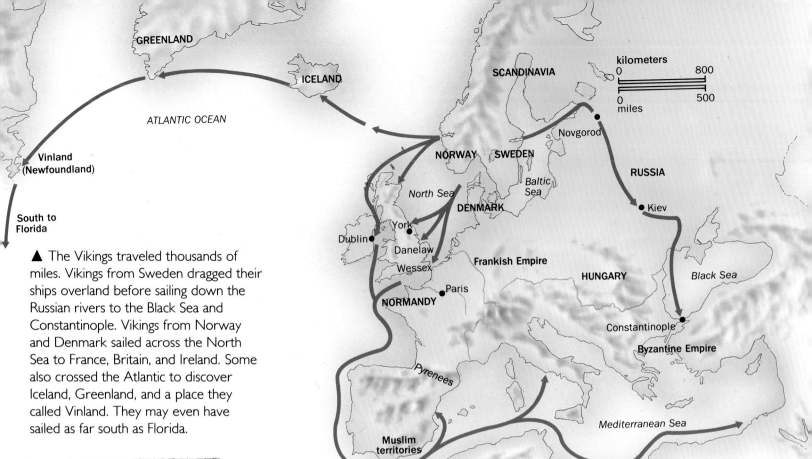

GREENLAND

ICELAND

ATLANTIC OCEAN

SCANDINAVIA

kilometers
0   800

0   500
miles

Novgorod

NORWAY   SWEDEN

RUSSIA

Vinland
(Newfoundland)

North Sea

Baltic
Sea

Kiev

South to
Florida

DENMARK

York

Dublin

Danelaw

Frankish Empire

HUNGARY

Black Sea

Wessex

Paris

Constantinople

NORMANDY

Byzantine Empire

Pyrenees

Muslim
territories

Mediterranean Sea

▲ The Vikings traveled thousands of miles. Vikings from Sweden dragged their ships overland before sailing down the Russian rivers to the Black Sea and Constantinople. Vikings from Norway and Denmark sailed across the North Sea to France, Britain, and Ireland. Some also crossed the Atlantic to discover Iceland, Greenland, and a place they called Vinland. They may even have sailed as far south as Florida.

▲ The Vikings excelled at metalwork. This die, used to stamp an identifying picture on a metal sheet, shows two legendary warriors about to attack a ferocious beast.

▼ The main reason for the success of the Vikings was the speed and seaworthiness of their longboats. The Vikings believed that the spirits of past leaders lived in the boats. For this reason, and because a boat provides safe passage to the land of the dead, they buried their leaders with their ships when they died. This longboat, made for a queen, was found preserved in mud at Oseberg, Norway.

▲ The Vikings could not read or write, so **sagas**, or legends, about their gods and heroes were learned by heart and handed down from parent to child by word of mouth. This wood carving shows the legendary hero Sigurd killing Fafnir the dragon.

Norman invaders

In 1066 Edward the Confessor, the king of England, died. He had no children to succeed him, and so three people claimed the English throne. They were Harold, earl of Wessex (who was Edward's choice as his successor); the king of Norway; and William, duke of Normandy, who was Edward's cousin and who claimed that Harold had once promised to support his claim to be king. Harold was crowned king, but immediately the other two **claimants** prepared to attack Harold and seize the throne.

The king of Norway was the first to attack. He sailed over the North Sea with an army and landed in the north of England. There he was quickly defeated by Harold and killed in battle. But then William landed with a large army on the south coast of England. William was a descendant of the Viking invaders of northern France who had settled there by 911 and had become known as Normans. Harold headed south to fight William's army but was defeated by them at a battle outside Hastings. William "the Conqueror" then marched to London and was crowned king of England on Christmas Day, 1066.

William set about controlling his new kingdom by building fortified castles and giving lands and titles to his Norman followers. He soon overcame English opposition and ruled securely until his death in 1087.

▲ The Bayeux Tapestry tells the story of the Norman invasion of England. The tapestry is more than 230 feet long and was made soon after the invasion in 1066. This section shows the Norman fleet crossing the English Channel.

◄ For four hundred years from 1066 the kings of England were also dukes of Normandy and acquired additional land in France through marriage. By 1154 they ruled over a greater area of France than the French king.

◄ In 1086 William the Conqueror ordered that a list be made of all the landowners in his new kingdom. The list took a year to compile, and the results were recorded in the Domesday Book. Domesday means "doomsday," or "day of judgment."

Castles

▲ Laying siege to a castle

The **baron**, or lord, of an area built a castle to defend the surrounding countryside, administer his lands, and provide a safe home for his family to live in. A castle was therefore a military barracks, an office, and a house. The castle was protected from attack by a moat full of water which could only be crossed by a drawbridge. This would be raised in times of danger. A high wall surrounded an inner courtyard where there were stables for horses and living quarters for soldiers. Local people could bring their animals into the courtyard if they were attacked. At the center of the castle stood the keep, a fortified house in which the lord and lady of the castle lived.

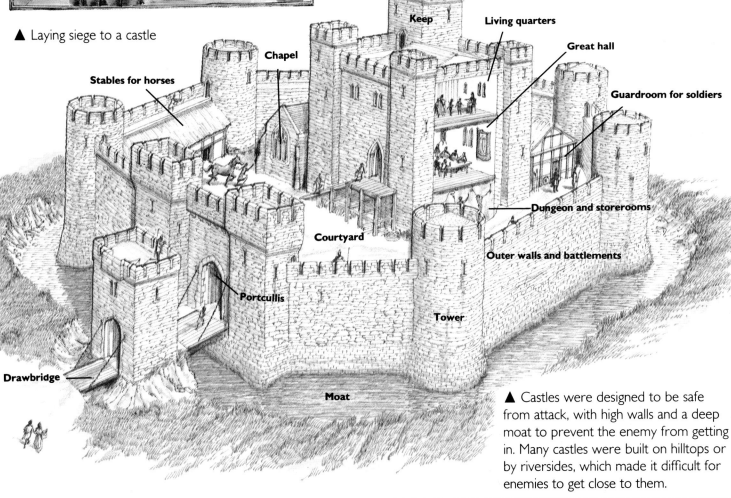

Keep

Living quarters

Great hall

Chapel

Guardroom for soldiers

Stables for horses

Dungeon and storerooms

Courtyard

Outer walls and battlements

Portcullis

Tower

Drawbridge

Moat

▲ Castles were designed to be safe from attack, with high walls and a deep moat to prevent the enemy from getting in. Many castles were built on hilltops or by riversides, which made it difficult for enemies to get close to them.

The Crusades

From about 200, Christian pilgrims from Europe traveled to Jerusalem and other parts of the Holy Land to worship in the places where Christianity had begun. But from 638 the Holy Land was controlled by Muslim Arabs. At first, the Muslims did not interfere with the pilgrims, but in 1071 the Turks conquered the area. They attacked the pilgrims and prevented Christians from worshiping in Jerusalem.

In 1095 Pope Urban II called on all Christians to go on **crusades** to the Holy Land to fight a holy war against the Turks. Within a year, a large army from all over Europe had gathered at Constantinople. When the crusaders reached the Holy Land in 1099, they captured Jerusalem and set up several Christian kingdoms in the area.

Nine Crusades were organized between 1147 and 1271, but none was as successful as the first.

Jerusalem was recaptured by the Muslims in 1187. Several Crusades tried to take it back; a Children's Crusade attempted to recapture it in 1212, but the children were not armed and most died or were sold into slavery before they reached the Holy Land. In 1291 the Christians were finally thrown out of the Holy Land.

The Crusades failed for many reasons. The crusaders were often poorly equipped, and they frequently quarreled among themselves. Many had gone to the Holy Land to make themselves rich, not to defend their religion.

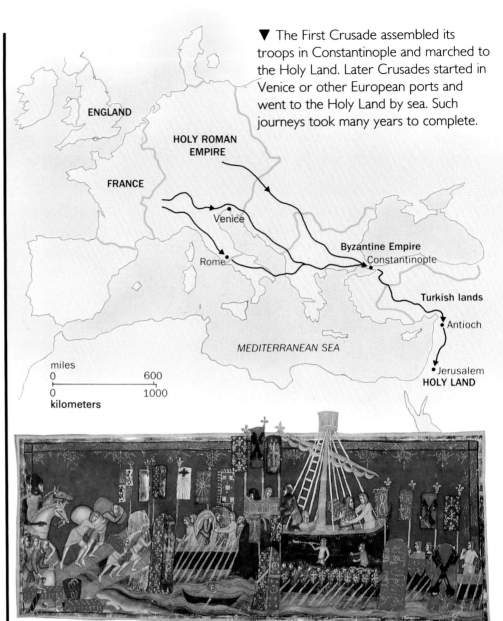

▼ The First Crusade assembled its troops in Constantinople and marched to the Holy Land. Later Crusades started in Venice or other European ports and went to the Holy Land by sea. Such journeys took many years to complete.

ENGLAND

HOLY ROMAN EMPIRE

FRANCE

Venice

Rome

Byzantine Empire
Constantinople

Turkish lands

Antioch

MEDITERRANEAN SEA

miles
0   600
0   1000
kilometers

Jerusalem
HOLY LAND

▲ Loading food and other supplies for a Crusade.

◀ Krak des Chevaliers (Castle of the Knights) in Syria was one of the strongest of the crusader castles, built to guard the routes from the East to the Mediterranean coast.

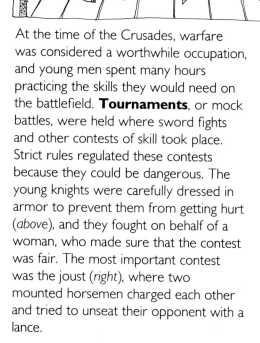

◀ A knight would consider the rescue of a damsel in distress to be a great honor. The highest duty of a knight was to protect vulnerable people.

▼ As part of the tournament, splendid banquets were held for the knights, lords, and ladies. After the meal the guests performed dances.

At the time of the Crusades, warfare was considered a worthwhile occupation, and young men spent many hours practicing the skills they would need on the battlefield. **Tournaments**, or mock battles, were held where sword fights and other contests of skill took place. Strict rules regulated these contests because they could be dangerous. The young knights were carefully dressed in armor to prevent them from getting hurt (*above*), and they fought on behalf of a woman, who made sure that the contest was fair. The most important contest was the joust (*right*), where two mounted horsemen charged each other and tried to unseat their opponent with a lance.

63

Empires Beyond Europe

The Maya people of America

The peoples of the American continent remained isolated, apart from the Vikings' brief visit to North America in 1003. Many ideas and inventions that were developed in Europe and Asia, such as the wheel and the plow, remained unknown in America. Instead, the Americans developed their own civilizations without any outside contact.

Between 300 and 900 the Mayas of Central America built a flourishing empire with huge cities dominated by massive temples, where they worshiped their gods. They were skilled astronomers and mathematicians and were the only American people who could read or write. Another major civilization was the city-state of Teotihuacán, where 250,000 people lived. The city covered five square miles and was one of the largest in the world, even bigger than Rome, then the largest city in Europe. Both the Mayan Empire and the city of Teotihuacán started to decline in about 750. In 900 the Mayans were replaced by the Toltecs as the greatest power in America. In 1200 the Toltecs themselves were replaced by the Aztecs.

The other great civilizations in America were in the Andes Mountains to the south. Up to 100,000 people lived there in the cities of Tiahuanaco and

▲ The great civilizations of Central and South America developed without any contact with the rest of the world.

◀ After about 900 the Anasazi people of the Mesa Verde, in what is now Colorado, built a series of **pueblos,** or communal houses. Each pueblo contained up to 800 rooms.

continued on page 66

◄ At the center of their cities the Mayas built pyramid-shaped temples surrounded by large palaces. This one is at Palenque, in Mexico. Thousands of workers were required to construct these buildings. Many thousands more worked in the fields nearby to provide food for the laborers.

▼ The Toltecs lived in Central Mexico and governed a large empire which traded throughout the region. In their capital, Tula, they built many temples, guarded by stone warriors like this one.

The Mayan language
The Mayas wrote in a picture alphabet that no one else understood (*below*). Only three of their documents survived the Spanish invasion in the 1530s. In the 1880s a scholar translated one document and began to decipher the Mayan language. However, many Mayan symbols are still not understood today.

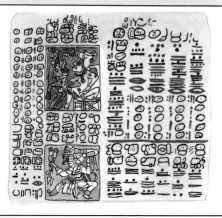

▲ The symbol of the cat appears throughout Central and South America on sculptures, carvings, pottery, and, as here, on a tapestry. In Peru, the city of Cuzco is thought to have been arranged in the shape of a puma.

65

Huari. Like the cities to the north, both Tiahuanaco and Huari were full of temples decorated with intricate carvings, and both were the capitals of powerful empires.

Trade in Africa

South of the Sahara a number of countries developed and grew rich on **commerce**, or trade. The kingdom of Mali controlled the trade that flowed along the Niger River and sold spices and gold to the Arabs who crossed the Sahara. The Arabs brought their Muslim religion with them, and gradually they converted the people of Mali and the neighboring areas to Islam. By 1300 the great trading cities of Djenné and Timbuktu were centers of Islamic learning and attracted scholars from all over western and northern Africa.

On the east coast of Africa, the ports of Kilwa and Gedi exported ivory, spices, and gold to Arabia, India, and China in return for carpets, ceramics, and horses. **Ambassadors** were sent to China to establish trading contacts, and fleets of Chinese **junks** visited the ports in 1418 and 1422, eager to buy the goods that were on sale.

Farther south, Great Zimbabwe was a wealthy state that grew rich on gold mining and cattle herding. The gold was taken overland to Sofala, where it was traded for beads, porcelain, and other luxuries with the Arab traders who sailed south down the eastern coast of Africa.

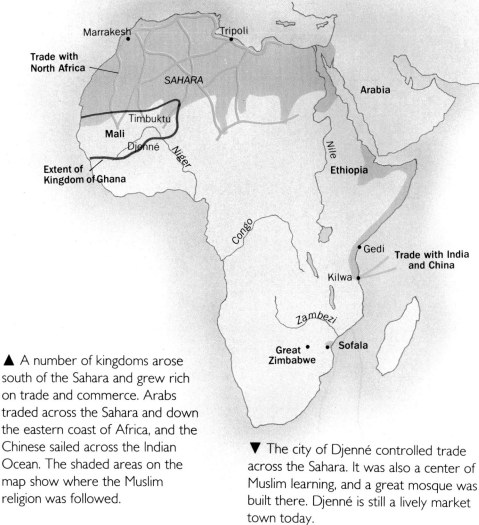

▲ A number of kingdoms arose south of the Sahara and grew rich on trade and commerce. Arabs traded across the Sahara and down the eastern coast of Africa, and the Chinese sailed across the Indian Ocean. The shaded areas on the map show where the Muslim religion was followed.

▼ The city of Djenné controlled trade across the Sahara. It was also a center of Muslim learning, and a great mosque was built there. Djenné is still a lively market town today.

450–1450

▲ The cities of eastern Africa, such as Kilwa, conducted trade across the Indian Ocean with India and China. In 1414 eastern African ambassadors visited the Chinese emperor with gifts, including a giraffe.

▼ Great Zimbabwe was the capital of a major trading empire that dominated southern Africa in the 1300s. The gold, iron, and copper mined in the region were much in demand throughout Africa. Many of the ruins of the huge defensive walls and towers of the city can be seen today.

▲ The only practical way for Arab traders to cross the vast and inhospitable Sahara was by camel. Groups of traders traveled together for safety. These groups were called caravans. Some camels were ridden, but many others were used to carry the traders' heavy loads. Although jeeps and trucks have now largely replaced them, camels are still used today for transportation.

▲ Ethiopia was the only Christian country in Africa. By 1200 the kings of Ethiopia had constructed 11 churches out of solid rock. The church of St. George at Lalibela is shaped like a cross and, like the other 10 churches, is still in use today.

Mongol invasions

The Mongols were tribes of nomads from the steppes, or plains, of central Asia. The different tribes often quarreled among themselves, and it was not until 1206 that one of their leaders, Temüjin, was proclaimed supreme ruler. He took the name Genghis Khan, which means "universal ruler" or "invincible prince," and his forces soon began to conquer the surrounding countries.

In 1211 the Mongols invaded northern China and captured Beijing, its capital, in 1215. They then turned west and by 1223 had conquered central Asia. Genghis Khan died in 1227, but his son Ogotai continued the conquests in Russia, Hungary, and on the shores of the Adriatic Sea. The Mongols had an army of 150,000 men, and there was no power in Europe capable of stopping them. But then Ogotai died, and the Mongols retreated.

Under their new leader Mangu, they captured Baghdad in 1258 and would have overrun the rest of the Islamic world had not Mangu also died. His successor was Kublai Khan, who was less warlike and spent his life uniting the vast country of China. He allowed the Mongol Empire to break up into smaller sections.

At its height in 1279, the Mongol Empire stretched from the Pacific Ocean almost to the Baltic Sea, and from the Persian Gulf to the Arctic Circle. It was the biggest empire the world had ever seen.

▲ The Mongols were excellent riders and were able to cover up to a hundred miles a day on their small and speedy horses. They fought with sharp arrows that could penetrate armor.

▼ In 1271 the Venetian traveler Marco Polo left Venice to visit China. He stayed in China for 20 years and met Kublai Khan, its ruler. Below is an illustration from the book he wrote about his travels. It shows gifts being presented to "the Great Khan."

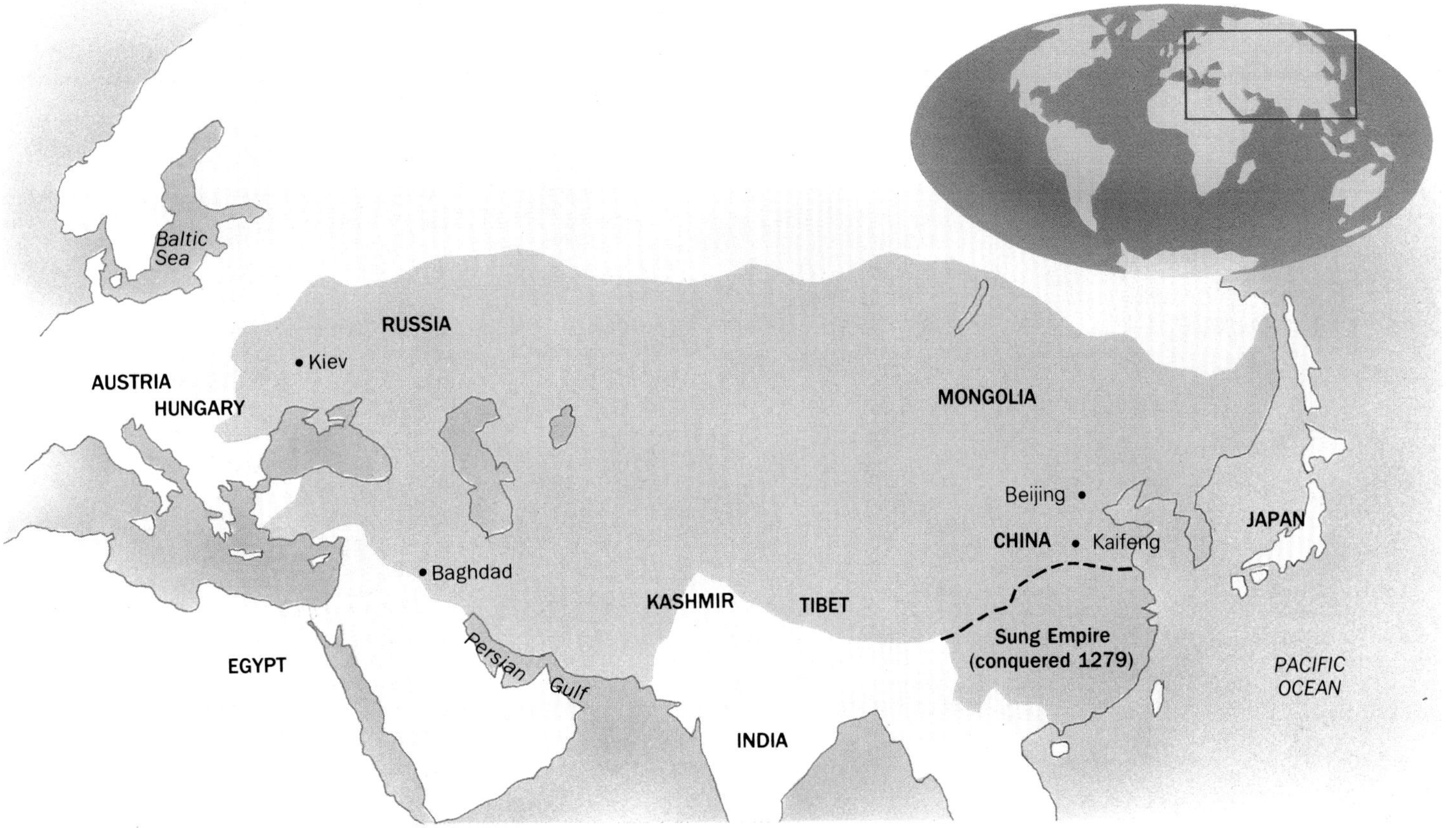
Baltic Sea
RUSSIA
Kiev
AUSTRIA
HUNGARY
MONGOLIA
Beijing
JAPAN
CHINA
Kaifeng
Baghdad
KASHMIR
TIBET
Sung Empire
(conquered 1279)
EGYPT
Persian Gulf
PACIFIC OCEAN
INDIA

▲ The Mongol Empire was the largest empire the world had ever seen. At its greatest extent it stretched across Asia into eastern Europe and sent expeditions of conquest into Austria, Egypt, India, Java, and Japan.

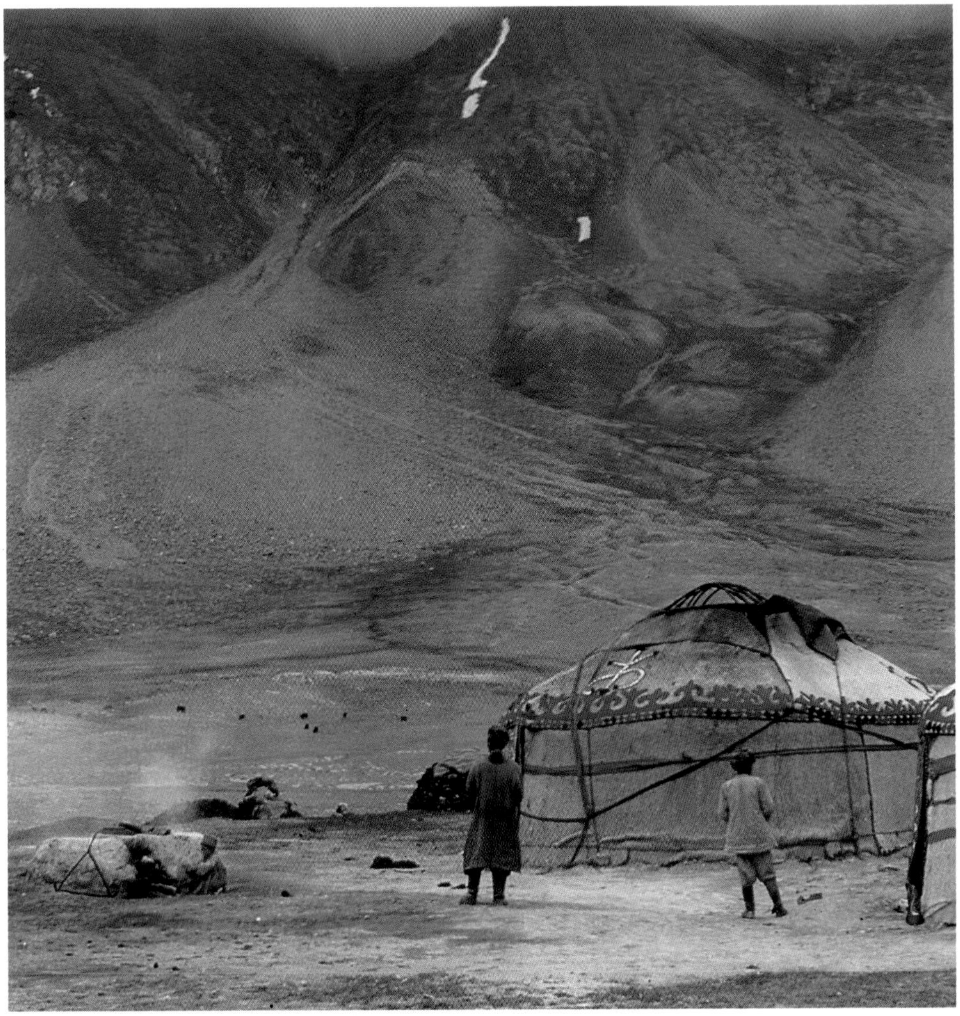

◀ The Mongols lived in yurts, or tents. The yurts were made of skins or woven cloth stretched over a wooden frame, and they were decorated with brightly colored rugs. They may not look strong, but they were warm enough to keep out the cold of winter. Some tribes in Mongolia and Afghanistan still live in yurts today.

The Growth of Trade

Wars in Europe

In 1200 Europe was divided quite differently from the way it is today. Spain was divided into four separate countries, one of which, Granada, was ruled by the Moors of northern Africa. Some areas of France were ruled by the kings of England, and Germany, the Netherlands, Switzerland, Austria, and northern Italy were all part of the Holy Roman Empire. Italy was divided into many small city-states, while in eastern Europe the constant wars meant that the borders of the countries were always changing.

The most powerful ruler in western Europe was the **pope** As the head of the Roman Catholic Church, the pope ruled over the wealthiest organization in western Europe. The Church had vast amounts of land, with estates in many different countries, and nearly everybody was a member of the Roman Catholic Church. The pope therefore had great influence over how the various European countries conducted their affairs.

This vast power brought the pope into conflict with the Holy Roman emperor, who claimed to be the leader of western Europe. The pope had the right to crown the emperor and used this right to assert his superiority over the emperor and all other rulers. But the

continued on page 72

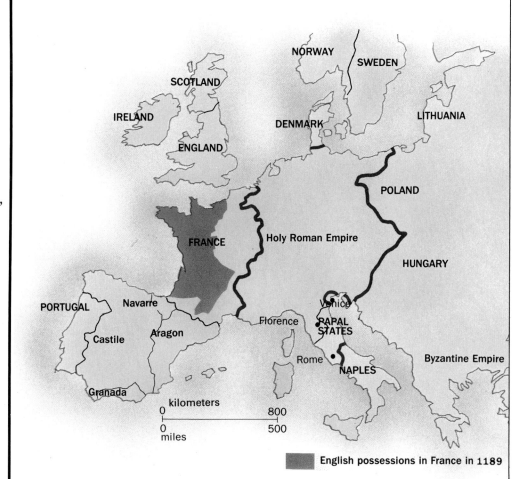

English possessions in France in 1189

▲ In 1200 Europe was a patchwork of different states that were often at war with each other. The Holy Roman Empire consisted of numerous small states held together by the Holy Roman emperor and the pope. Quarrels between these two powerful rulers dominated European history at this time.

▶ In order to govern their countries better, many European kings summoned parliaments. These meetings were composed of nobles and other high-ranking people from each town. They levied (collected) taxes on behalf of the king and helped him administer the country. The English parliament (*right*) was summoned by Edward I in 1295 and consisted of two knights from each county and two representatives from each town.

The Black Death

The Black Death

The Black Death was a plague spread by fleas, which lived on both rats and humans. No one knows where the plague started, but it was probably brought from Asia into Europe by rat-infested ships that traded across the Mediterranean. The plague arrived in Sicily in 1347 and then spread slowly northward throughout the rest of Europe, reaching Scandinavia by 1353. Its effect was devastating. Almost everyone who caught the plague — perhaps one third of the total population of Europe — died. Whole towns and villages were wiped out and harvests were left to rot in the fields. Only a few areas were unaffected, because they managed to isolate themselves and prevent the rats from spreading the disease.

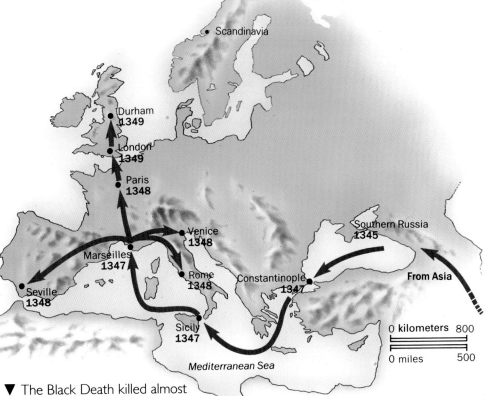

▼ The Black Death killed almost everybody who caught it. It was often portrayed in pictures of the time as a dead person riding a horse, killing both rich and poor as it swept across the land.

▲ The Black Death probably came from Asia to Europe in 1347. It was carried by fleas that lived on rats and on humans.

The Peasants' Revolt

Many other disasters struck Europe after 1300. A series of bad harvests led to widespread famine. Outbreaks of smallpox and influenza killed many people. Food prices rose because there were fewer people working on the land to produce the food. Across Europe, peasants demanded higher wages, and violent demonstrations broke out in many countries. The most serious was in England, where wages were kept low by law. In 1380 taxes were increased and many peasants revolted. Led by Wat Tyler, the peasants marched on London in 1381 and demanded changes in their working conditions. But Wat Tyler was killed and the revolt was brutally put down.

emperor wanted to be independent of the pope. As a result, the two frequently quarreled and at times fighting broke out between them.

Daily life

The quarrel between the Holy Roman emperor and the pope had little impact on the daily lives of most men and women. For them, the most important thing was to produce enough food to eat.

At this time, almost everybody lived and worked on the land under a system known as the **feudal system**. The term "feudal" comes from a Latin word meaning "fief," or piece of land. The feudal system began in France in about 750 and soon spread across Europe. Each king granted land to his most powerful barons or lords, who swore an oath of loyalty and agreed to fight for the king. The barons then divided this land into manors.

The lord of the manor gave **villeins,** or peasants, strips of land to farm for themselves, but in return they had to work in their master's fields and give him some of their produce each year. This system of land management was called manorialism. The peasants grazed pigs and grew crops such as wheat and beans.

The feudal system survived in Russia and eastern Europe until the 1800s. In western Europe, however, it began to collapse in the 1300s when more and more people began to work in the towns where the feudal system did not apply.

▲ The first modern European bank was established in Venice in 1171 in order to lend money to the government. Banks were soon formed in every major European city, for they helped develop trade and commerce. Merchants used the banks to deposit and invest their money safely.

◀ The most important building in people's lives was the church. Everyone went to church, and the local priest was often the most important member of the community. In bigger towns and cities, cathedrals were built to show off the wealth and power of the church. These cathedrals took many years to build and employed numerous local craftworkers. Stonemasons, wood carvers, and glassmakers all helped decorate the cathedral with sculptures and colored glass.

► Harvesting was a laborious task, requiring every man, woman, and child to help. The barley or rye that was harvested went to make bread for the peasants, who also lived on eggs, cheese, milk, and the occasional chicken or pig. The nobles ate much better and used wheat for their bread.

▼ In this gold and silver mine in central Europe, the miners are shown wearing white so that they can be seen in the dark. Above ground people crush and wash the minerals while others sell them (*top*) under the supervision of royal controllers.

▼ In the bigger houses, servants were employed to cook and clean. This lady of the manor is giving orders to her kitchen staff.

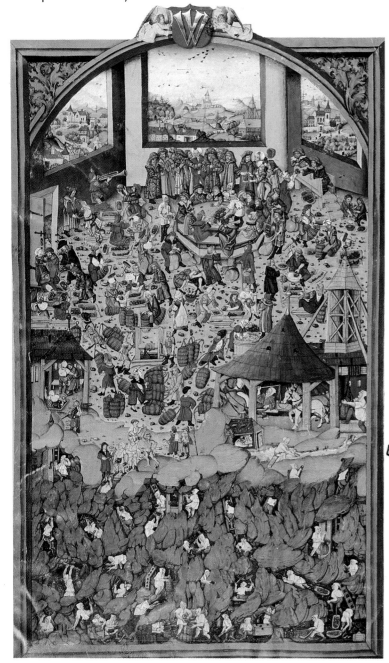

▼ Lepers and disabled people begging for food were common sights in many towns and villages.

The Hanseatic League

In Europe, towns only started to grow in size after about 1200 when the threat of nomadic invasions had gone. New towns grew up along trade routes where roads met or rivers could be crossed, and old towns expanded in the shadows of great cathedrals or fortified castles. These towns grew rich on trade. Many of them held fairs or markets where merchants could buy and sell their goods. Groups of craftworkers, such as goldsmiths or carpenters, formed associations known as **guilds** to protect their craft and train apprentices in their skills. These guilds grew rich and contributed much to the wealth of the towns.

In northern Europe, trade was dominated by the German towns around the south shore of the Baltic Sea. But this trade was often threatened by pirates at sea and robbers on land. In 1241 two of the towns, Hamburg and Lübeck, agreed to protect each other's merchants and safeguard their trade routes by setting up a *hanse*, or trading association. By 1300 all the German ports had set up hanses. Together they formed the Hanseatic League to safeguard their trading interests.

In 1400, at its greatest extent, the Hanseatic League had more than 150 members and traded throughout northern Europe. The Hanseatic traders brought copper, iron, and herrings from Sweden, and furs, grain, and timber from eastern Europe and Russia. To the east, the

continued on page 76

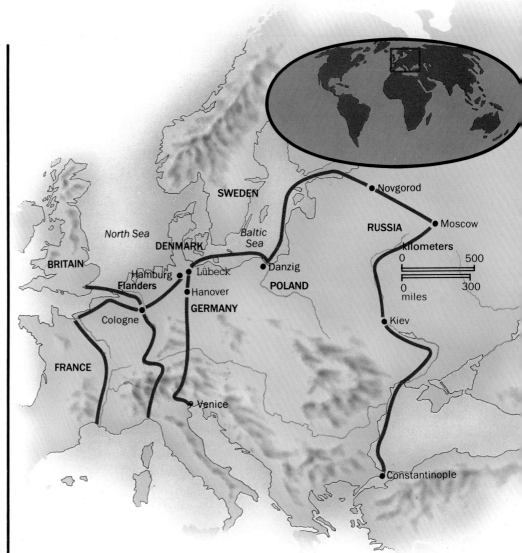

▲ Trade routes of the Hanseatic League, the most important trading association in Europe. Its member towns stretched from Russia to Flanders and controlled trade in both the North and Baltic seas.

▼ In the 1400s the fortified city of Novgorod, in Russia, was an important trading center of the Hanseatic League. Amber, furs, and wax were all traded here.

74

1200–1450

Inventions and Technology

Inventions came about over the course of many years as new ideas were used to improve old methods of working. Many of these inventions developed in China over hundreds of years and then slowly made their way to Europe, often through Arab influences. But printing and gunpowder remained unknown in Europe for many years after their first use in China, while the Chinese armies had no knowledge of the deadly longbow used by the English.

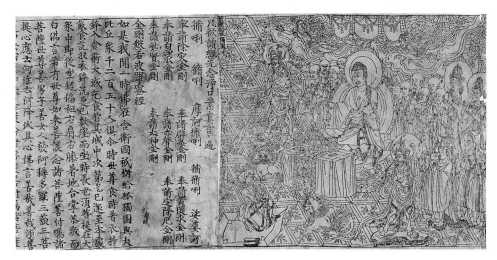

▲ The Diamond Sutra was printed in China in 868 and is the oldest surviving printed book in the world. The book is a collection of Buddhist prayers.

◄ The longbow was developed in England in the 1200s and was a lethal weapon because of the speed and accuracy of its delivery.

▼ The padded horse collar, a Chinese invention, was introduced into Europe in the 900s. It enabled horses to be used on farms to pull heavy loads. Here a horse wearing a padded collar is pulling a harrow.

▼ The Chinese were skilled ironworkers. Here a group of workers are forging a ship's anchor in the 1300s.

merchants or traders of the League controlled the town of Novgorod, in Russia, and dominated trade in that country. To the west, they traded across the North Sea with England. There the traders were known as Easterlings because they came from the east. In time the word became shortened to "sterling" and referred to the money the Hanse traders used. The word "sterling" is still in use today as the name for British currency.

Southern Europe

Venice was the most important trading city in southern Europe. As early as 900, the Venetians controlled most of the trade with the Middle East and China. They profited by equipping the fleets and armies that went on the Crusades, and by 1400 Venice had established an empire of trading ports throughout the eastern Mediterranean Sea. In this way it became the richest city in Europe.

China

In China too, towns were growing in size and importance. The population of China had reached over 110 million people by 1100, many more than lived in the whole of Europe. Cities such as Kaifeng (see map on page 69) became important trading and industrial centers, and by 1450 China had become the richest and most organized country in the world.

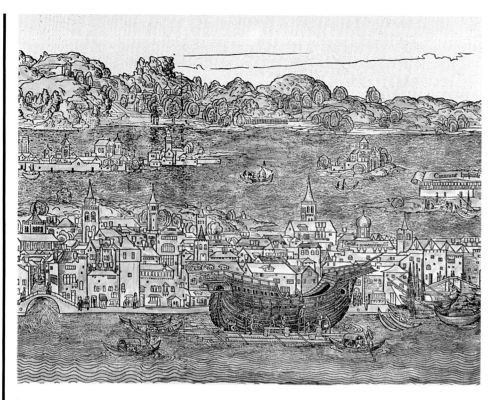

▲ For many years traders to the Middle East and China started their journeys from Venice. By 1400 it was a thriving port and the richest commercial city in Europe.

▼ Between 960 and 1127 the Chinese capital was at Kaifeng. It had a population of perhaps one million people and was a major center of trade and industry. This scroll, drawn in about 1120, shows the bustle of the annual spring festival.

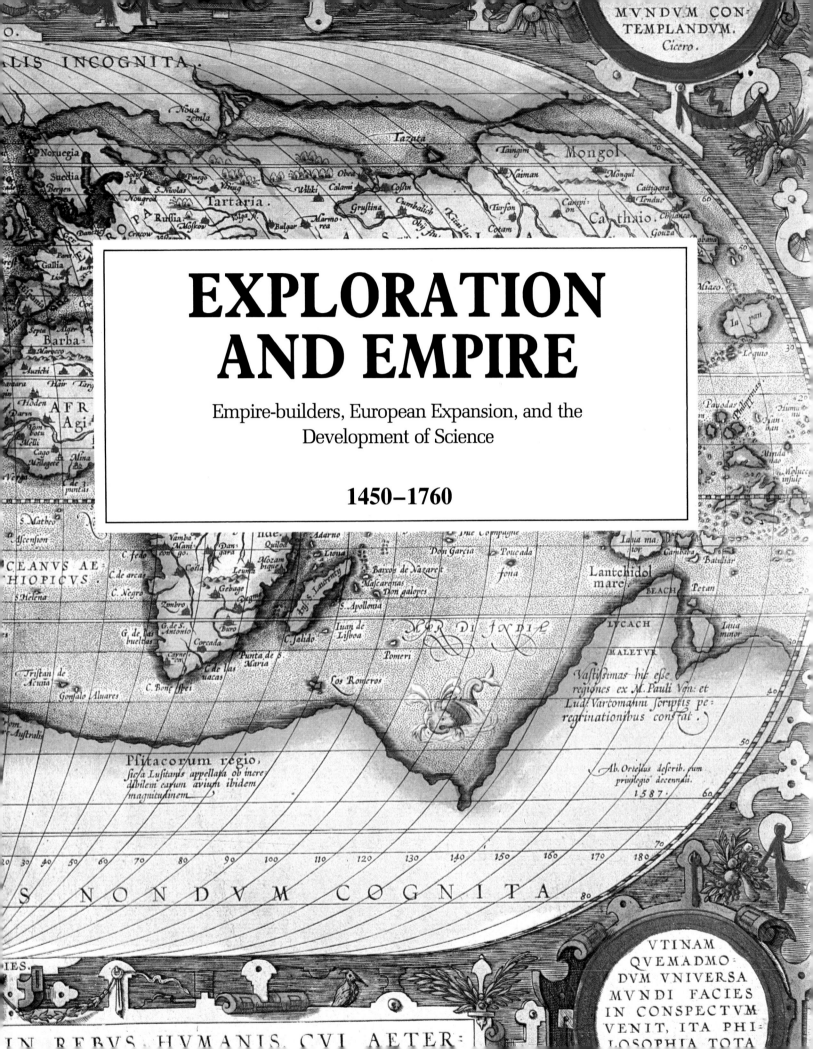

EXPLORATION AND EMPIRE

Empire-builders, European Expansion, and the
Development of Science

1450–1760

Old and New Horizons

Old and new

Today we live in a world of fast travel and instant communication. But in 1450 most people never traveled farther than their own town or village. Others did not know that countries existed beyond their own. Great civilizations rose and flourished almost independently of each other.

Western Europe, which influences so much of our lives today, was on the edge of the civilized world in 1450. All around the world, civilizations such as the Mogul Empire in India, the Ming dynasty in China, and the brilliant Aztec and Inca empires in Central and South America flourished. In West Africa the kingdom of Benin rose to its height, and in Australia the Aboriginal culture continued to thrive as it had done for many thousands of years, independent of any contact with the outside world.

Toward one world

But the world was poised on the brink of great change. Between 1450 and 1750 European seafarers, traders, and colonists set out to explore and exploit the rest of the world. This brought the continents into direct contact with each other for the first time. From 1450 the history of the world begins to move from

continued on page 80

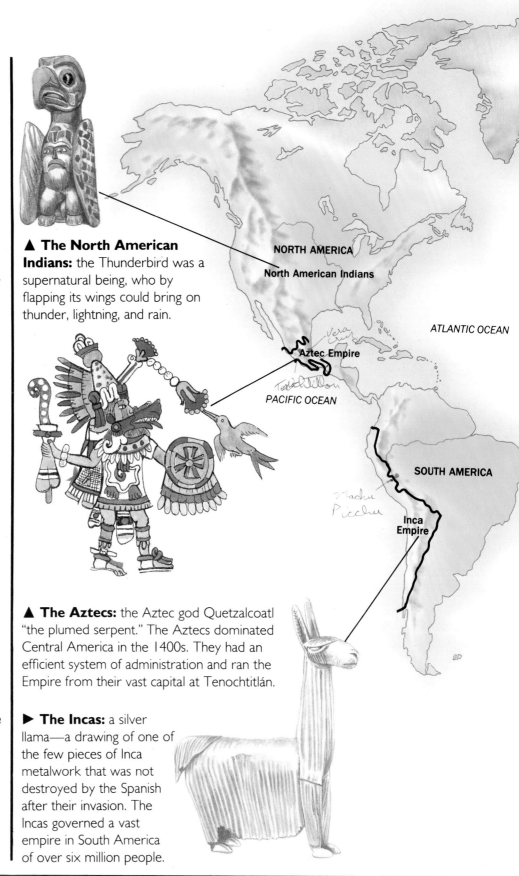

▲ **The North American Indians:** the Thunderbird was a supernatural being, who by flapping its wings could bring on thunder, lightning, and rain.

▲ **The Aztecs:** the Aztec god Quetzalcoatl "the plumed serpent." The Aztecs dominated Central America in the 1400s. They had an efficient system of administration and ran the Empire from their vast capital at Tenochtitlán.

▶ **The Incas:** a silver llama—a drawing of one of the few pieces of Inca metalwork that was not destroyed by the Spanish after their invasion. The Incas governed a vast empire in South America of over six million people.

78

1450

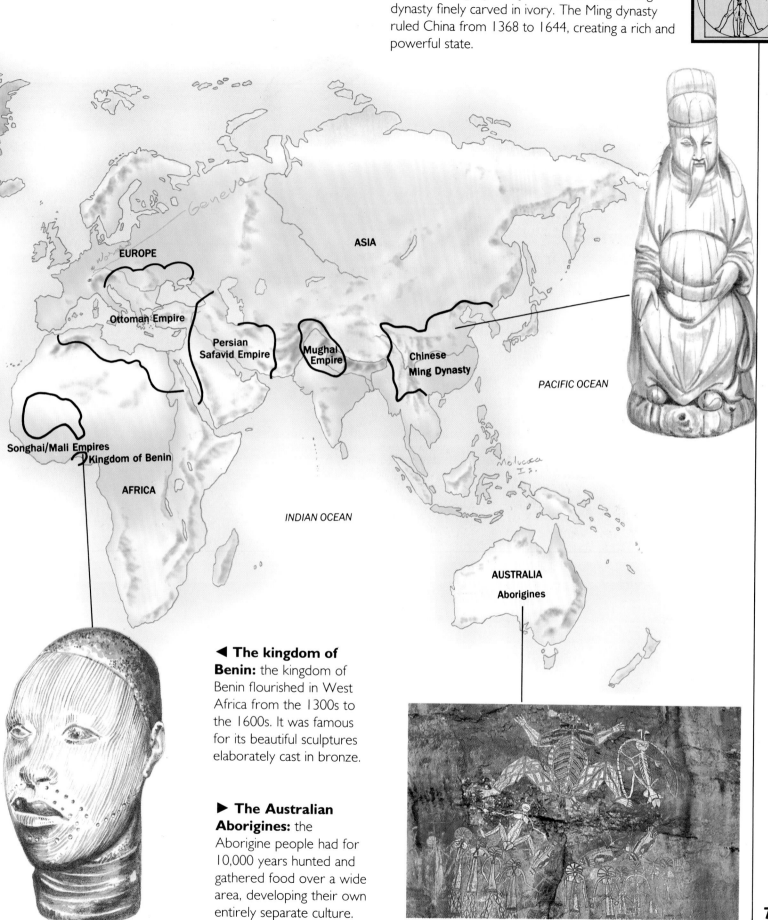

▶ **The Ming dynasty:** an official of the Ming dynasty finely carved in ivory. The Ming dynasty ruled China from 1368 to 1644, creating a rich and powerful state.

EUROPE

ASIA

Ottoman Empire

Persian
Safavid Empire

Mughal
Empire

Chinese
Ming Dynasty

PACIFIC OCEAN

Songhai/Mali Empires
Kingdom of Benin

AFRICA

INDIAN OCEAN

AUSTRALIA
Aborigines

◀ **The kingdom of Benin:** the kingdom of Benin flourished in West Africa from the 1300s to the 1600s. It was famous for its beautiful sculptures elaborately cast in bronze.

▶ **The Australian Aborigines:** the Aborigine people had for 10,000 years hunted and gathered food over a wide area, developing their own entirely separate culture.

79

being the story of different civilizations to the history of one interconnected world.

New ways of thinking

As we have seen, Europe in 1450 was not the richest or the most important region of the world. But it was a place where important changes were occurring. During the 1400s and 1500s there were great advances in the arts and sciences, and the beginnings of new and exciting ways of thinking about the world and human nature.

This period in European history is called the **Renaissance** (meaning *rebirth*). It began in northern Italy where wealthy and educated people began to take a renewed interest in the art and literature of ancient Greece and Rome. This led to great achievements by artists such as Raphael, Michelangelo, and Leonardo da Vinci. People also became interested in learning and in a new spirit of inquiry, influenced by ideas from the Islamic world. The science of astronomy was developed, and there were advances in medicine. Scholars and thinkers began to challenge the rigid teachings of the medieval Church.

Helped by the invention of printing, the ideas and scholarship of the Renaissance gradually spread throughout Europe. The Renaissance only affected the wealthiest and most privileged in society, but it provided a stimulus to the European urge to explore and discover the world outside the Mediterranean area.

▶ The Renaissance started among the many city-states of northern Italy. Here, art and architecture were paid for by wealthy and educated people, including women like Isabella d'Este (*below*), who took a personal interest in the new learning.

◀ Leonardo da Vinci was a painter, sculptor, architect, and engineer. Among his many drawings was an idea for a flying machine, devised 400 years before the first aircraft, and this parachute.

• Milan
Verona
Padua
• Venice
• Mantua
Modena •
• Bologna
• Ravenna
• Pisa
• Florence
• Urbino
• Siena

ITALY

■ Rome

| 0 | 50 miles |
| 0 | 50 kilometers |

▲ The city of Florence was one of the main centers of the Italian Renaissance, with many rich **patrons** supporting artists and architects.

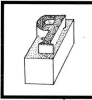

The Invention of Printing

Today we take newspapers and books for granted. But until the 1450s information was either passed from one person to another by word of mouth or copied and written out by hand. In the 1450s a German craftsman, Johannes Gutenberg, introduced the printing press into Europe. It revolutionized communication. For the first time books or "broadsheets" could be produced quickly and easily, which meant that more people than ever before had access to learning and ideas.

The Bible and classic Greek and Roman works were the first books to be printed in Europe. By 1520, there were more than 200 different printed editions of the Bible in several different languages. Printing was also used to spread the new scientific and political ideas of the Renaissance.

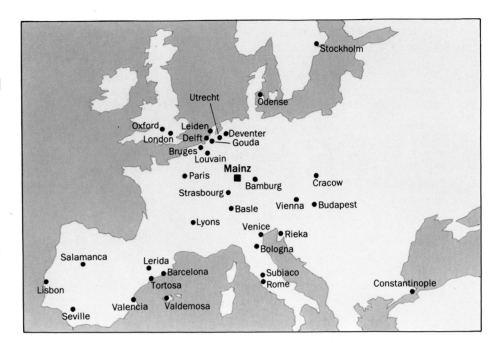

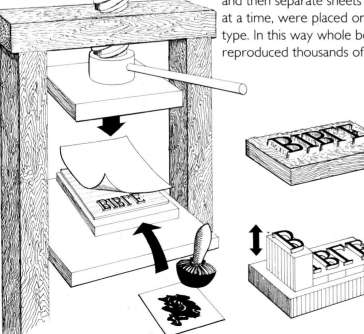

▼ Gutenberg's press, which was adapted from a wine press of the time, used movable metal type for the first time. Earlier printers carved groups of letters onto a woodblock; but Gutenberg's individual letters were cast in molds and could be moved and used over and over again. The type was inked, and then separate sheets of paper, one at a time, were placed on top of the wet type. In this way whole books could be reproduced thousands of times.

▲ The first European printing press was set up by Gutenberg in Mainz, Germany, in 1454. Over the next 50 years printing presses were introduced into Germany, Italy, France, Spain, and England.

▲ The *Ladies Mercury*, one of the early broadsheets, was printed and distributed widely.

Exploration and the Scramble for Riches

From around 1450, European sailors and navigators set out on remarkable voyages of exploration. Curiosity was one reason, the search for trade and wealth was another.

Overland trade routes had existed between Europe and Asia for centuries, along which merchants had brought spices, silks, and gems from the East to Europe. But in 1453 when the Ottoman Turks captured Constantinople (Istanbul), direct land links between Europe and Asia were cut completely. It became essential to find a sea route to the East.

In the 1460s the Portuguese explored the west coast of Africa, setting up forts and trading in gold, ivory, and silver. In 1488 Bartolomeu Dias reached the Cape of Good Hope. In 1498 Vasco da Gama was the first European to reach India by sea.

A "new world"

While the Portuguese were sailing east, the Spanish were exploring the oceans to the west. In 1492 Christopher Columbus set off to find India by sailing west. He was the first European to explore the Caribbean islands and, believing them to be part of Asia, called them the West Indies. He went on to find South America, an unknown continent.

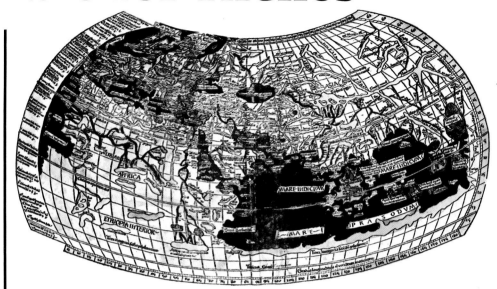

▲ Claudius Ptolemy drew his map of the world in the A.D. 100s, and it was rediscovered by Europeans in the 1400s. Using this map, the first Europeans to reach America believed that it must be part of Asia because the new continent was not on the map.

▶ The European exploration of the world was made possible by a new and faster type of ship, the caravel, developed by the Portuguese. Nevertheless, sailing into the unknown was a frightening experience, and many sailors believed that monsters would threaten them while at sea.

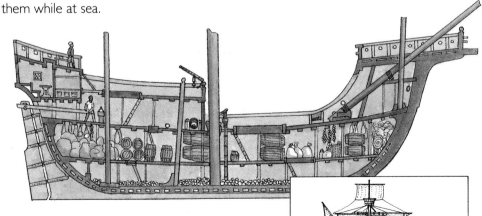

▲ Columbus's ship, the *Santa Maria*. Life aboard the *Santa Maria* was very tough—there were no sleeping accommodations for the crew, and their food was cooked in an open pot on deck.

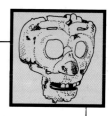

Amerigo Vespucci explored the South American coast down to the mouth of the Amazon. The previously unnamed continent in the **"New World"** was called America after him.

Between 1519 and 1522 **Ferdinand Magellan** proved that the world's oceans were linked by sailing around the world—but only 18 of his crew of 250 survived the voyage.

In 1498 **Vasco da Gama** became the first European to sail to India, in a voyage that took him around the coast of Africa.

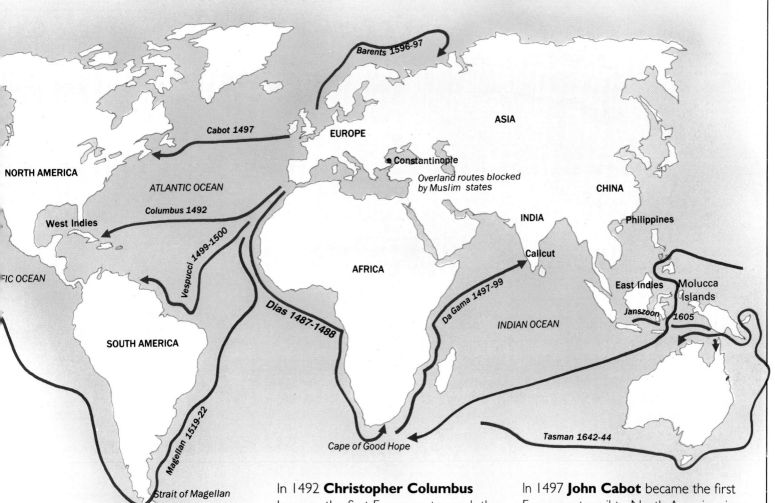

Barents 1596-97

Cabot 1497

EUROPE

ASIA

NORTH AMERICA

ATLANTIC OCEAN

Columbus 1492

West Indies

● Constantinople

Overland routes blocked by Muslim states

CHINA

INDIA

Philippines

FIC OCEAN

Vespucci 1499-1500

AFRICA

Calicut

East Indies

Molucca Islands

Dias 1487-1488

Da Gama 1497-99

Janszoon 1605

INDIAN OCEAN

SOUTH AMERICA

Magellan 1519-22

Tasman 1642-44

Cape of Good Hope

Strait of Magellan

Cape Horn

In 1492 **Christopher Columbus** became the first European to reach the Caribbean, landing in the West Indies. He later explored the South American coast.

In 1497 **John Cabot** became the first European to sail to North America since the Vikings, 500 years before. He explored Newfoundland and Canada.

Cheng Ho
Almost a century before the Europeans sailed into the Indian Ocean, the Chinese Ming rulers sent seven expeditions to explore this area. Commanded by Cheng Ho, vast fleets explored as far afield as East Africa, the Red Sea, Persia, India, and Java. They brought back gifts from the local rulers, rare spices, and unusual animals, including lions and giraffes.

Compass

Astrolabe

Backstaff

▲ Navigation at sea was a very primitive affair in the 1500s. The most important instrument was the compass, which showed in which direction the ship was sailing. The **astrolabe** and backstaff used the sun to calculate the ship's distance north or south of the equator. Sailors had no accurate way of finding out how far east or west they were until the mid-1700s.

83

Gold, guns, and disease

Explorers and navigators were followed by **conquistadors** and colonists in search of land and gold for their countries. The Spanish first occupied the Caribbean and then turned their attention to South and Central America, which were rich in gold and silver.

When the Spanish arrived in Central and South America they found two great civilizations—the Aztecs of Mexico and the Incas of Peru. Both were highly organized societies of millions of people. The Aztecs had developed astronomy, methods of irrigation, and a highly diverse agriculture of crops such as corn, tobacco, and tomatoes, which the Europeans later took back to Europe. Both the Aztecs and Incas were highly skilled builders. Tenochtitlán, the Aztec capital which lay on Lake Texcoco, was larger than any European city of the time. Yet between 1519 and 1534 both empires were overthrown by the Spanish conquistadors and their wealth and land seized.

The Spanish conquest was achieved by Hernán Cortés, who overthrew Aztec rule between 1519 and 1521, and by Francisco Pizarro, who conquered the Inca Empire between 1532 and 1534. Although the Spanish were few in number, they brought guns and horses against which the American peoples had no defense. As a result, the Spanish were able to capture the Aztec and Inca leaders very easily.

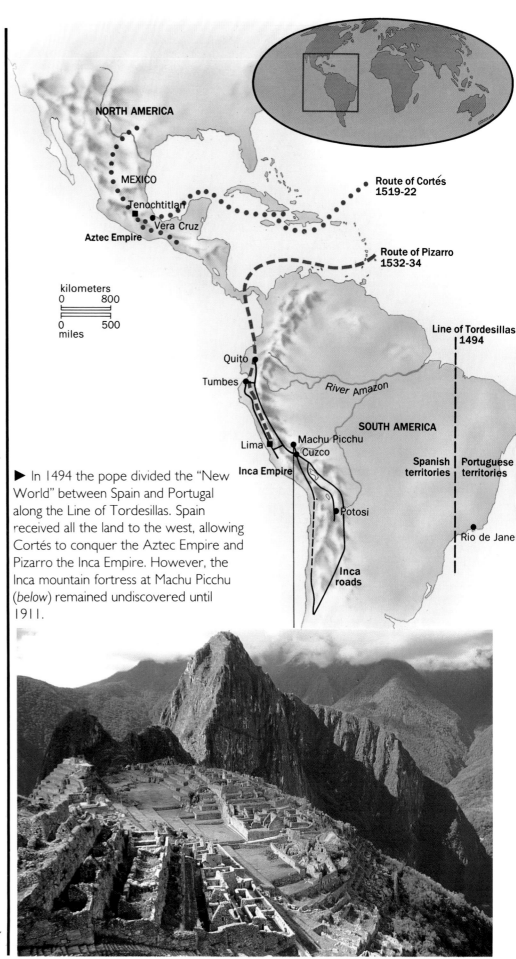

► In 1494 the pope divided the "New World" between Spain and Portugal along the Line of Tordesillas. Spain received all the land to the west, allowing Cortés to conquer the Aztec Empire and Pizarro the Inca Empire. However, the Inca mountain fortress at Machu Picchu (*below*) remained undiscovered until 1911.

▲ In order to exploit the gold and silver of the "New World," the Spanish put the Native Americans to work in the mines. Conditions were harsh and many thousands died.

▶ When the first Europeans arrived in the Aztec Empire in 1519, its ruler Montezuma believed them to be gods and welcomed them into the capital, showering them with gifts.

◀ This snake, made of hollow wood covered with turquoise, was made by Aztec craftspeople and probably sent as a tribute to Tenochtitlán. It was worn at the back of the head as part of a headdress.

When the Spanish began to conquer South America in 1519, the native population was about 57 million. By 1607, this had dropped to just over 4 million. Some of this decline was due to warfare and harsh conditions in the mines, but much of it was because of the introduction of European diseases, such as measles, smallpox, and chickenpox, against which the native peoples had no **immunity**.

▼ The central part of the great Aztec city, Tenochtitlán. The city was begun in 1325 and built on an island on Lake Texcoco.

Temple of Huitzilopochtli

Priests' quarters

Sacrificial skull rack

Temple of the Sun

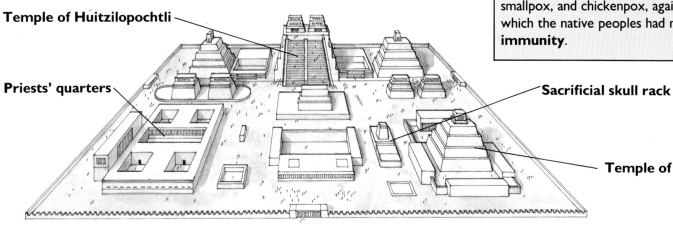

The scramble for riches

By the mid-1550s the Spanish and Portuguese had established the first European overseas empires. They set up **plantations** in the Caribbean and colonized large areas of South America. In 1510 the Portuguese captured Goa in India. In the 1540s they became the first Europeans to land in Japan. By the 1550s they controlled trade in the Indian Ocean and the **Spice Islands**. But from the late 1500s onward the **Netherlands**, France, and England began to challenge Spain and Portugal and to compete with them for trade in spices and slaves.

England was already a great sea power and trading nation. As well as trading for slaves in the Caribbean, English pirates and sailors such as Francis Drake raided the Spanish colonies in the Americas, plundering their ships and carrying off gold, silver, and other treasure. In 1588 Philip II of Spain sent an armed fleet — the **Armada** — to attack England, but the Spanish fleet failed in its task. This weakened Spain's empire and led to the growth of British power overseas.

The Dutch too were a prosperous nation. They drove the Portuguese out of the Spice Islands, and in 1658 they captured Ceylon (Sri Lanka). By the 1680s they had built up their own empire in Southeast Asia. By 1650 the European nations had established a sea-trading network that stretched as far as India.

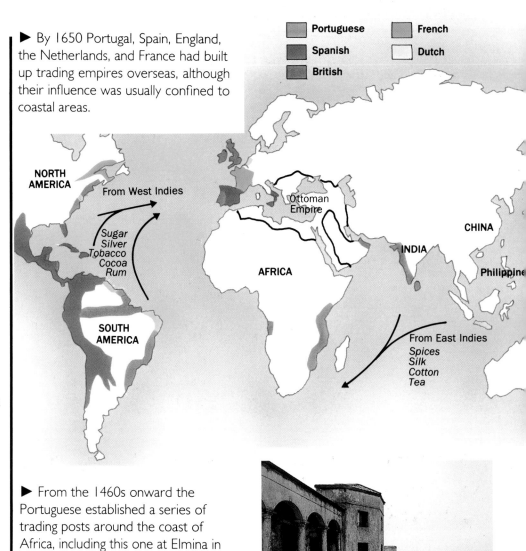

▶ By 1650 Portugal, Spain, England, the Netherlands, and France had built up trading empires overseas, although their influence was usually confined to coastal areas.

Portuguese
Spanish
British
French
Dutch

▶ From the 1460s onward the Portuguese established a series of trading posts around the coast of Africa, including this one at Elmina in West Africa.

▼ The European invasion of the "New World" was often opposed, and the local peoples continued to fight the invaders for years. In 1608 the native **Caribs** of St. Lucia fought against the British colonists.

1450–1650

The Spice Trade

When the Portuguese reached the East Indies in the early 1500s, they found the islands rich in spices unobtainable in Europe. The Portuguese quickly took control of this lucrative trade by conquering the Moluccas, or Spice Islands, and seizing the main ports in the Indian Ocean and China through which the spice trade passed.

For almost a century, the Portuguese controlled the spice trade with Europe, but by 1600, both England and the Netherlands had established East India Companies to obtain spices directly for themselves. The Dutch were the most successful, driving the Portuguese out of the Moluccas and keeping the English out of the region altogether. They encouraged the growing of tea, coffee, sugar, and tobacco on the islands, and by 1720 they had become the main coffee suppliers to Europe.

▲ Harvesting pepper cloves in the Spice Islands.

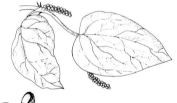

▲ Pepper is used to season food and flavor soups.

▲ Nutmeg is used to flavor custards and puddings.

▲ Cloves are used to flavor food, particularly meat.

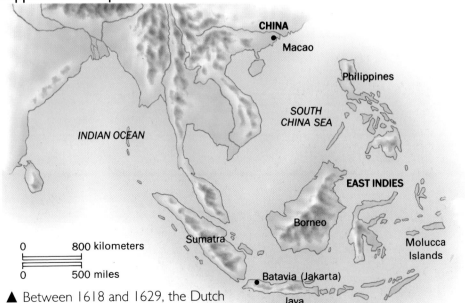

▲ Between 1618 and 1629, the Dutch expelled the Portuguese from the Spice Islands and established a vast empire with its capital at Batavia (Jakarta).

▲ Mace is used in pickles and hot mulled wines.

Religion and Change

In the early 1500s the Christian Roman Catholic Church was the main religion in Europe. The Church was the most powerful force in society: it dominated people's thinking. But within 50 years, almost half the population of western Europe had left the Roman Catholic Church to worship in rival Christian churches. This change is called the Reformation. It resulted from a protest about the corruption of the Roman Catholic Church and its priests, and a demand for reform.

In 1517, Martin Luther, a German monk, wrote a list of 95 "theses," or complaints, which were printed and circulated throughout Europe. The Church refused to consider reform and Luther was **excommunicated**, or expelled, from the Roman Catholic Church in 1520. Luther then set up his own reformed church in Saxony. Similar churches were soon established in the rest of Germany and northern Europe.

In order to regain control of Europe, in 1545 the Roman Catholic Church began to reform itself, in a movement called the Counter Reformation. The Counter Reformation led to bitter civil wars and a general European war, the Thirty Years' War, that lasted from 1618 to 1648.

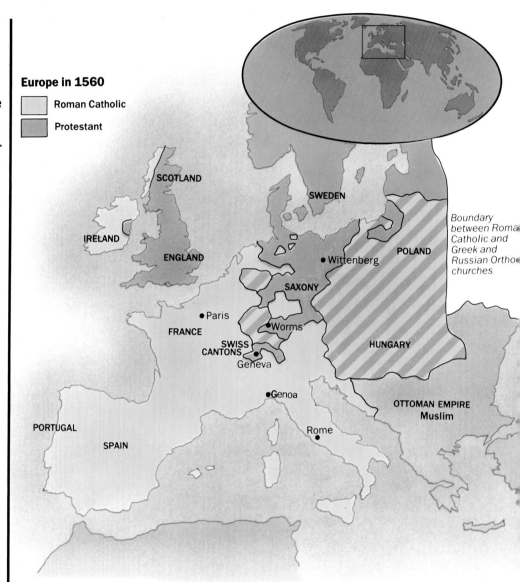

Europe in 1560
- Roman Catholic
- Protestant

Boundary between Roman Catholic and Greek and Russian Orthodox churches

SCOTLAND
IRELAND
ENGLAND
SWEDEN
POLAND
●Wittenberg
SAXONY
●Paris
●Worms
FRANCE
SWISS CANTONS
Geneva
HUNGARY
●Genoa
OTTOMAN EMPIRE Muslim
PORTUGAL
SPAIN
Rome●

▲ By 1560 the people of Europe were divided by their religion. Those who broke away from the power of the Roman Catholic Church are shown as Protestants on the map—in fact there were many different new movements, the Anglicans in England, the New Lutherans, and the Calvinists, for example. In the east the Russian and Greek Orthodox Christian churches had long been established, and in the southeast, the Ottoman Empire was Muslim in faith.

15 4 8

► Martin Luther. His followers were called Protestants because they protested against the Roman Catholic Church.

▼ Inside St. Peter's in Rome, the center of the Roman Catholic Church.

◀ The Calvinist Church was based on the severe and strict teachings of John Calvin, a Frenchman living in Geneva. Its buildings were stark in comparison with the decorative Roman Catholic churches.

▼ From 1562 to 1598, France was split by religious wars between Roman Catholics and Huguenots, or Protestants of the Calvinist Church. The Roman Catholic queen, Catherine de Medici, ordered all the Huguenots to be killed on St. Bartholomew's Day in 1572. Over 29,000 Protestants all over France were murdered.

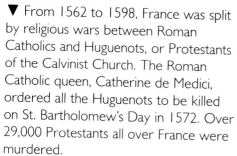

Henry VIII of England
In England, Henry VIII wanted to divorce his wife, Catherine of Aragon, because she had failed to produce a male heir to the throne. The Roman Catholic Church would not agree, so Henry made himself head of the new Anglican Church and granted his own divorce. He dissolved the monasteries, the richest landowners in the country, and seized their wealth, increasing his own power.

Rich and poor

In the 1500s and 1600s in Europe the vast majority of people lived off the land. Famine, poverty, and disease were common and few people lived past the age of 40. Most remained poor and uneducated, lacking the knowledge or equipment to farm efficiently. The weather and harvest were the most crucial aspects of their lives.

But changes were taking place that gradually altered people's lives. Between 1500 and 1700 the population of Europe grew steadily, leading to pressure for more efficient and productive farming. In some countries, such as England, wealthy local landowners began to enclose open fields and **common land** in order to make higher profits — they turned **arable** land into pasture for sheep, and threw the peasant farmers off the land.

In the towns, rich merchants were profiting from increased trade and commerce throughout Europe and with the rest of the world. With their newfound wealth they invested their money in the new banks set up to finance the growing **merchant economy**. Many rich people were also commissioning fine buildings and works of art, particularly in the Netherlands, which by 1650 was the richest country in Europe. The growth of the new merchant class, dedicated to business and profit, meant that by 1650 the gap between rich and poor had become very wide.

▲ The first plows had a single wedge, tipped with iron, that could only break the surface of the soil, not turn it. By the middle of the 1600s double plows were in use throughout Europe. These new plows were able to turn the soil and to prepare it better for planting the crops.

▼ Most people who lived in the 1500s and 1600s were poor, living on the land and dependent on a good harvest for their livelihood. This painting by Pieter Breughel shows the living room of a Flemish farmer in the early 1600s. A rich nobleman and his wife bring presents of salt and money to the farmer's family.

The potato
In 1500, the potato grew in the Andes Mountains of South America, and the only people who ate it were the Incas. Their Spanish conquerors introduced it into Europe in the middle of the 1500s, but it was about 200 years before it became the popular food in Europe that it is today. In about 1600, the potato was taken back across the Atlantic by settlers who introduced it to North America.

Nuns, Witches, and Dissenters

▲ The Quakers were a religious group which began in the mid-1600s in England. They were also known as the Society of Friends. They believed that men and women were equal. This picture shows a woman preaching.

Life was hard for most women during this period because by law women had few rights. Their lives and their fortunes were controlled by their fathers or, if they were married, by their husbands. Most women worked in the fields and brought up many children.

Some unmarried women entered convents as nuns. In 1535 one nun, Angela Merici, founded a teaching order, the Ursulines, who later emigrated to North America and set up the first convent in Quebec in 1639. Other older women were herbalists, who tended the sick in the villages. Many people were suspicious of these women, who suffered and were persecuted as witches from the 1400s through the 1700s. 1400s through the 1700s.

Women also played some part in the political and social changes of the time. In Italy and France a number of notable women, such as Lucrezia Borgia and the artist Artesemia Gemileschi, played a leading role in the new learning. By the 1600s, some women were beginning to demand women's rights. In England during a time of political and religious dissent in the 1640s a pamphlet appeared. It was called *The Women's Sharpe Revenge*. Written by two women who called themselves Mary Tattle-well and Joan Hit-him-home, it attacked the critics of women and was an early demand for women's rights.

▼ In Europe from the 1400s through the 1700s, thousands of women were accused of being witches and were tortured and burned as a result. Most of the women were healers or wise women who used ancient herbal remedies to cure sicknesses, and whose beliefs clashed with the new science of the time.

▼ Noblewomen did have certain traditional rights in the 1400s and 1500s, but from the 1600s onward these were gradually taken away. Lady Anne Clifford was an English noblewoman who fought against the loss of these rights.

The Ottoman Empire

To the east of Europe lay one of the largest and most successful empires in the world—the Ottoman Empire. It had been founded by Muslim Turks in the late 1200s. Under their king, Osman I, from whom the empire took its name, the Ottomans managed to exploit the weaknesses and divisions of their neighbors and establish dominance over Anatolia (Turkey) and then farther afield in Europe, Asia, and Africa. Their greatest triumph came in 1453 when they captured the great Christian city of Constantinople, capital of the Byzantine Empire.

They renamed this city Istanbul and made it the capital of their vast empire. At its greatest extent in 1566, the Ottoman Empire covered almost a million square miles, from Algeria to Arabia and from Budapest to Cairo. In 1529 and again in 1683, the Ottomans even reached the capital of the Holy Roman Empire, Vienna, in the heart of Europe, but were unable to capture it.

Throughout most of the 1500s, the Ottoman Empire was at war with its neighbor, the Safavid Empire of Persia (Iran). Like Christian Europe, the Muslim world was divided—the Ottomans were of the Sunni sect and the Safavids were Shi'ites, and the two sects fought many wars on religious grounds. This dispute still continues today.

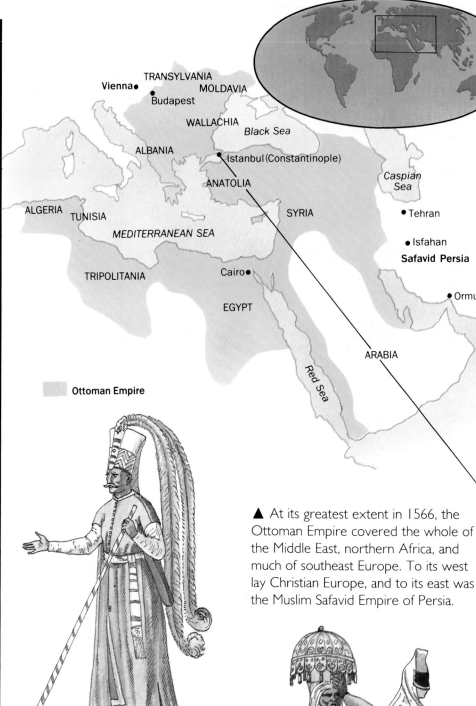

Ottoman Empire

▲ At its greatest extent in 1566, the Ottoman Empire covered the whole of the Middle East, northern Africa, and much of southeast Europe. To its west lay Christian Europe, and to its east was the Muslim Safavid Empire of Persia.

In order to fight their many wars, the Ottomans had a highly trained army led by Janissaries (*above*). Distinguished by their tall plumed hats, these elite troops were Christians, captured or recruited from Europe. Ottoman women, however, were considered little better than the servants employed by each rich household. This Turkish lady and her servant are on the way to the baths (*right*).

92

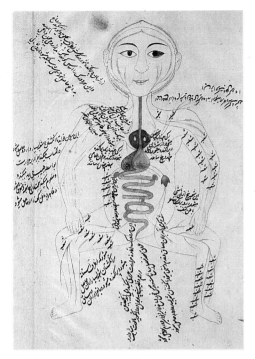

▲ The study of medicine was very advanced in the Islamic world. This Persian manuscript of the 1600s shows an understanding of the human organs and the circulation of the blood.

▶ Sultan Suleiman I brought Ottoman power to its peak when he brought his armies to the gates of Vienna. He is seen here at the Battle of Mohács in 1526, when he defeated the Hungarian army. *Upper center:* Suleiman rides his horse through a pile of dead bodies. *Lower corner:* defeated Hungarians flee on horseback.

After the capture of Constantinople in 1453, the Ottomans renamed the city Istanbul and made it their capital. Minarets were built onto the Christian church of St. Sophia, and it was turned into a mosque (*below and left*).

93

The Mogul Empire

At the same time that the Ottoman Turks and the Persian Safavids were establishing their empires, a third empire was being founded in India. All three were Islamic. Together they ensured that by the 1500s the Islamic world was far larger than the Christian.

The Islamic empire in India was founded in 1504 when a group of Turks led by the Muslim ruler Babur captured the city of Kabul in Afghanistan. Babur claimed to be descended from the Mongol ruler Genghis Khan; from the word "Mongol" came Mogul. Babur soon moved south into the fertile plains of northern India, and in 1526 his army of 12,000 defeated a 100,000-strong Indian army. Establishing their capital at Delhi, Babur and his successors took over most of India by the mid-1600s.

Although the Moguls were Muslims, four fifths of their subjects were Hindus, who were at first allowed to practice their religion freely. But by the 1700s, the Hindus were being persecuted, leading to strains within the Empire that eventually led to its breakup.

A further threat came from the fact that the Moguls had never had much interest in the sea or overseas trade, so that Europeans, notably the Portuguese, were able to establish trading ports around the coast as early as 1510. These ports soon developed into bases for European powers seeking to expand their trade.

▲ In 1650, at the height of its power, the Mogul Empire covered almost all of present-day India, Pakistan, and Bangladesh. Many of its coastal towns were occupied by Europeans, particularly the Portuguese, Dutch, French, and English.

▲ Although the Moguls were Muslims, they tolerated other religions within their empire, notably Sikhism. The Golden Temple in the city of Amritsar is the holiest shrine of the Sikh religion.

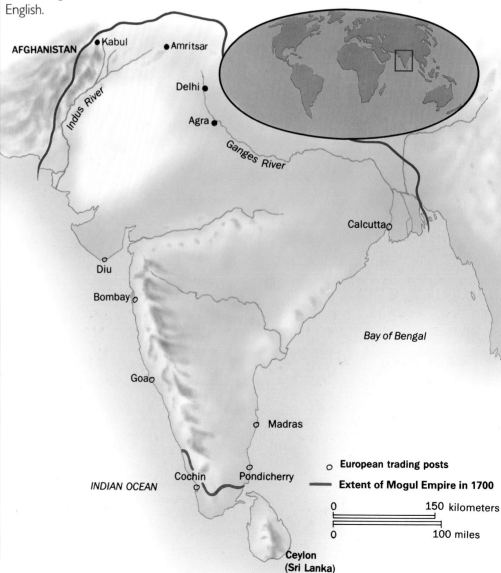

The first European settlements in India were founded not by countries but by trading companies, such as the British East India Company. Set up in 1600 with a charter from Elizabeth I of England to trade with the East, the British East India Company soon acquired many privileges from the Moguls, such as employing local women (*above*) to produce cotton for export and planting large estates with tea (*right*) to satisfy the British thirst for the drink.

▼ When Babur became Mogul emperor, he complained that India had no grapes, no good fruits, and no cold water. He therefore encouraged the building of beautiful gardens.

▼ Built as a mausoleum (tomb) for Mumtaz, the favorite wife of Emperor Shah Jahan, the Taj Mahal took 20,000 builders 18 years to complete. It was finally ready in 1648.

95

Slavery and the "New World"

A hundred years or so after Columbus arrived in the Americas, people from all over Europe began to cross the Atlantic to settle in what they called the New World. The Portuguese and Spanish concentrated on Central and South America and the Caribbean. There they mined for silver and set up vast plantations which were worked by slave labor, growing profitable crops, such as tobacco, sugar, and cotton.

The French, Dutch, and British concentrated on North America. In 1535 Frenchman Jacques Cartier sailed up the St. Lawrence River and established a port at Montreal in what is now Canada. French influence then extended into central North America, which the French called Louisiana after their king, Louis XIV.

In 1607 the British set up their first permanent American colony at Jamestown in Virginia. They continued to colonize the Atlantic coast, expelling the Dutch from New York in 1664, and by 1700, more than 250,000 English people were living in North America. They organized their settlements into 12 colonies. The thirteenth, Georgia, was formed in 1733. These 13 colonies eventually formed the first states of the United States of America.

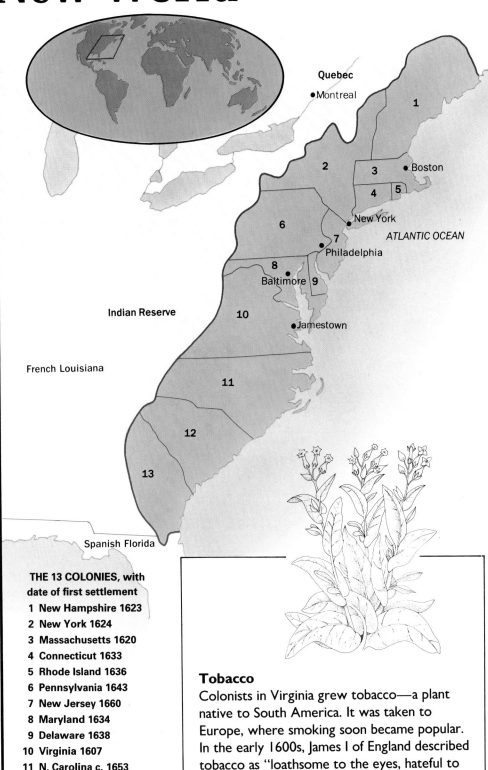

THE 13 COLONIES, with date of first settlement
1 New Hampshire 1623
2 New York 1624
3 Massachusetts 1620
4 Connecticut 1633
5 Rhode Island 1636
6 Pennsylvania 1643
7 New Jersey 1660
8 Maryland 1634
9 Delaware 1638
10 Virginia 1607
11 N. Carolina c. 1653
12 S. Carolina 1670
13 Georgia 1733

Tobacco
Colonists in Virginia grew tobacco—a plant native to South America. It was taken to Europe, where smoking soon became popular. In the early 1600s, James I of England described tobacco as "loathsome to the eyes, hateful to the nose, harmful to the braine, dangerous to the lung . . ."

A chief Heroroans wyfe of Pomeoc and her daughter of the age of 8. or 10. yeares.

▲ Some native tribes of North America lived by hunting and trapping wild animals for their fur and meat. In this picture two Native Americans camouflage themselves in order to stalk their prey. At first this way of life was unaffected by the arrival of the Europeans. But gradually the two groups came into bitter conflict as the Native Americans were driven from their land by the expanding European colonies.

▶ One of the first settlers in North America was John White, a mapmaker and artist who drew pictures of the Native Americans, including this one of a woman and her child.

Many of the first European colonists were dissenters, people who disagreed with the accepted religion in their country and who were persecuted for their beliefs. One of these groups, the Pilgrims, was made up of Puritan men and women who disagreed with the English Anglican Church. They left England in 1620 on the *Mayflower* (*above*) and founded a settlement in Massachusetts.

A PURITAN FAMILY.

Settlers and Americans

The early European settlers found existing cultures already established on their arrival in the "New World." At that time North America contained many different tribes of Native Americans, each with their own customs and ways of life. The first settlers met with little opposition, as their small numbers posed no threat to the local inhabitants, whom they named "Indians." The settlers needed the Indians to supply them with food and furs to supplement the unreliable deliveries from Europe and to help them through the harsh winters and years of crop failure. At the same time, the Indians wanted to acquire arms to fight their local wars.

Local **alliances** soon sprang up. In Canada in 1649, the French helped one Indian tribe, the Iroquois, destroy another, the Huron, and farther south similar alliances were forged between the British settlers and local Indian groups. These alliances divided the Indians and prevented a united Indian threat to the fledgling colonies.

European settlers soon outnumbered the Indians, and relations between the two groups worsened. In 1637 British colonists in Connecticut killed between 600 and 700 Pequot Indians and all the New England colonies were involved in a war against the Wampanoag and Narraganset Indians in 1675–1676, which led to the virtual destruction of tribal life in the area.

▲ The first European settlers built themselves simple log cabins able to withstand the cold winters they encountered in the "New World." But as they established themselves, they cleared more land and built bigger and more comfortable houses.

▼ Many Native Americans were experienced in trapping wild animals, especially beavers, for their skin and fur, which they traded with the European settlers for arms and other goods.

▼ In 1612 the Dutch settled on an island in the Hudson River and named the place New Amsterdam. When the English captured it in 1664, they renamed it New York. This map was drawn in 1664 and shows the English fleet in the harbor.

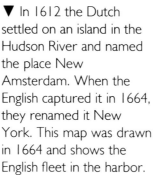

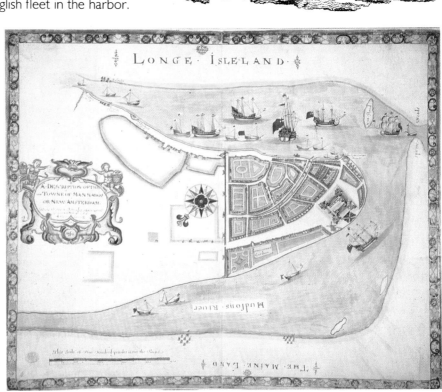

LONGE ISLELAND

The Slave Trade

Between the 1400s and 1800s at least 10 million black Africans were shipped from Africa to labor on the sugar, tobacco, and cotton plantations of the Caribbean and North America. The Portuguese were the first to practice this trade in human lives; later the British became the main slave traders. In a horrendous but profitable **"triangular trade,"** ships sailed from Britain with manufactured goods which were exchanged for slaves on the west coast of Africa. Cargoes of slaves—women, men, and children—were taken across the Atlantic (the "middle passage") and then sold in the Caribbean and North and South America, where most were worked to death on the plantations. The same ships then took the products of the plantations—cotton, raw sugar (known as white gold because it was so profitable), and tobacco—back to Europe, where they were sold.

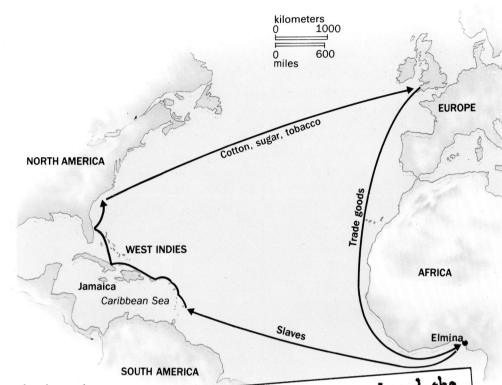

◀ Many black Africans rebelled. The fighting **Maroons** of Jamaica were escaped slaves who, in 1738, forced the British to make a **treaty** with them.

▼ During the middle passage from Africa to the Americas hundreds of black Africans were crammed together on disease-ridden slave ships and transported across the Atlantic in appalling conditions. Many perished.

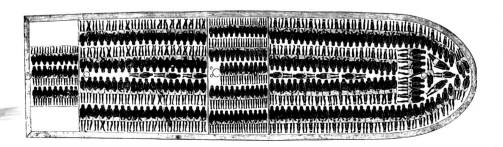

Africa

By the 1500s the African continent was home to many different political states and powerful kingdoms. Within the continent these societies had developed trade networks, advanced forms of agriculture, gold mining, cloth working, and a variety of crafts and skills. Contact between these states and the rest of the world was limited, for the Sahara Desert in the north was an almost impassable barrier to all but the hardiest of traders. But the gradual spread of Islam across the desert linked Africa more closely to the Arab world, and by the 1600s, trade between Africa and the Mediterranean was established.

Europe and the slave trade

The arrival of Europeans interrupted African development. At first European settlement was limited to coastal areas as the Portuguese began to trade with West African kings for gold, ivory, pepper, and cloth in exchange for various goods, most of which were of little use to the Africans. Slaves also formed part of this trade. At first, European demand for slaves was met by West African states where slavery existed as punishment for various crimes. But by the 1700s Europeans were buying or kidnapping slaves from the whole of Africa. The effect on African cultures was devastating, and by the late 1700s the population had declined and many African states were seriously weakened.

BRANDING SLAVES,
ON THE COAST OF AFRICA PREVIOUS TO EMBARKATION.

▲ When a slave was captured, he or she was branded, as described in a contemporary French account, "with a red-hot iron, imprinting the mark of the French, English, or Dutch companies, so that each nation may distinguish its own. Care is taken that the women, as tenderest, be not burnt too hard."

▶ An ivory carving from West Africa depicting Portuguese soldiers in a miniature ship's crow's-nest.

▼ Built on an island off Tanzania, the town of Kilwa became the major trading port in East Africa in the 1200s, with many houses of stone and mortar,

surrounded by orchards and fruit gardens irrigated by fresh water. In 1505 the Portuguese captured the town and built a fort to control it.

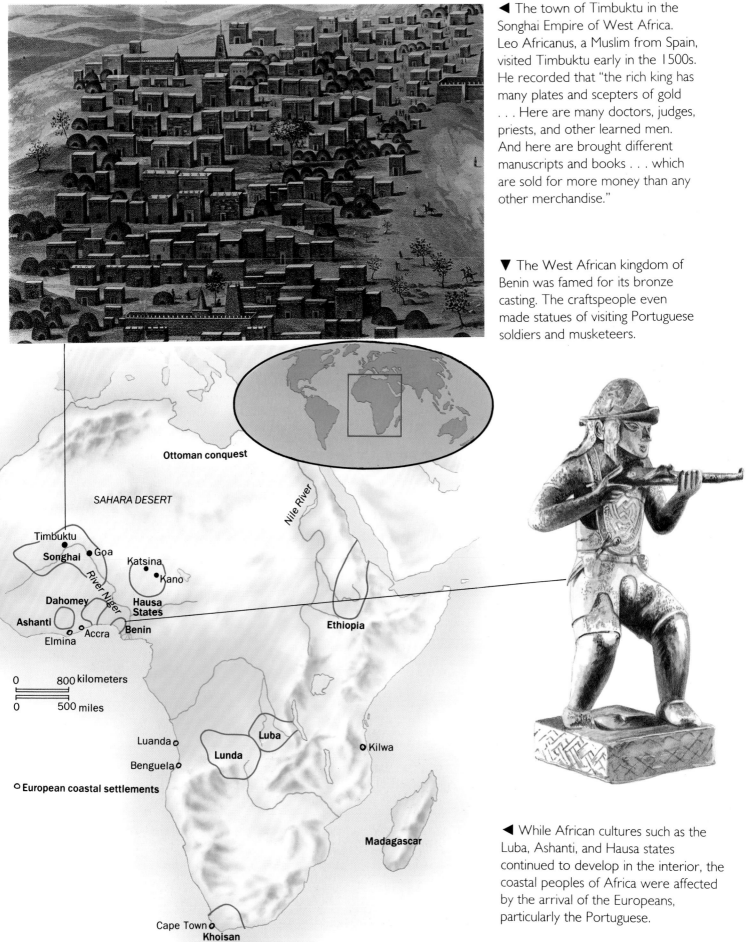

◄ The town of Timbuktu in the Songhai Empire of West Africa. Leo Africanus, a Muslim from Spain, visited Timbuktu early in the 1500s. He recorded that "the rich king has many plates and scepters of gold . . . Here are many doctors, judges, priests, and other learned men. And here are brought different manuscripts and books . . . which are sold for more money than any other merchandise."

▼ The West African kingdom of Benin was famed for its bronze casting. The craftspeople even made statues of visiting Portuguese soldiers and musketeers.

Ottoman conquest

SAHARA DESERT

Nile River

Timbuktu
Songhai ● Goa
● Katsina
● Kano
Dahomey River Niger **Hausa States**
Ashanti ○ Accra **Benin**
Elmina
Ethiopia

0   800 kilometers
0   500 miles

○ **European coastal settlements**

Luanda ○
Lunda **Luba**
Benguela ○
○ Kilwa

Madagascar

Cape Town ○
Khoisan

◄ While African cultures such as the Luba, Ashanti, and Hausa states continued to develop in the interior, the coastal peoples of Africa were affected by the arrival of the Europeans, particularly the Portuguese.

Struggles for Power

In 1648, a treaty called the Peace of Westphalia brought to an end the Thirty Years' War between the Catholic **Hapsburg** emperors and their Protestant subjects in the Holy Roman Empire. It also marked an important turning point. Until 1648, European wars had been fought mainly on religious grounds. Now different nations began to struggle among each other for political supremacy in Europe, and for trade and colonies abroad.

Between 1667 and 1714 France was involved in four major wars. At first these wars were to secure French frontiers in the east. But in 1700, when Charles II, king of Spain, died, it appeared possible that either Austria or France would take over Spain—with its possessions in Italy, the Netherlands, and the Americas—and thus dominate Europe. Alliances between different European countries were formed to support the two rival claimants to the throne, and this led to what is called the War of the Spanish Succession. It lasted from 1701 until 1714 and involved all the major nations of Europe. It was the first major war fought to maintain what is known as a "**balance of power**," in which no single nation has more power than another.

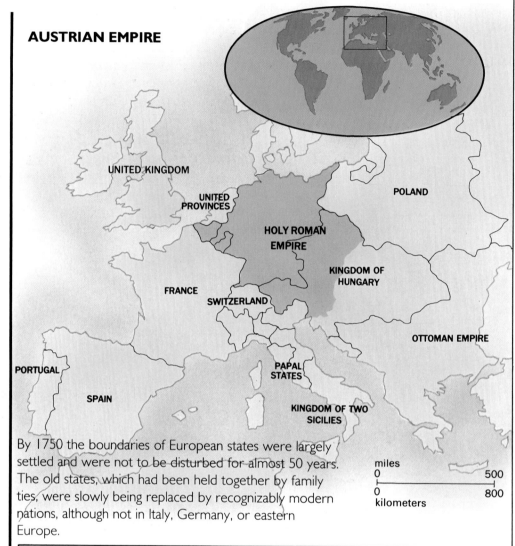

AUSTRIAN EMPIRE

By 1750 the boundaries of European states were largely settled and were not to be disturbed for almost 50 years. The old states, which had been held together by family ties, were slowly being replaced by recognizably modern nations, although not in Italy, Germany, or eastern Europe.

miles
0 — 500
0 — 800
kilometers

The English revolution

There were many different causes of the English civil war: its origins lay in the **authoritarian** behavior of the Stuart family of kings, who threatened the powers of the Parliament. Religious differences were important too: the Puritans in Parliament suspected the Stuart kings of Roman Catholic sympathies. Civil war broke out in 1642 and was resolved by the execution of King Charles I in 1649. For the next 11 years a republic was set up, the only one in British history, and the country was governed first by Parliament and then by Oliver Cromwell (*above*), an army leader. After Cromwell's death in 1658 Charles II returned from exile, and in 1660 was reinstated, but with his royal powers considerably reduced.

The Scientific Revolution

As a result of the Renaissance and Reformation, scientists began to question the idea that all knowledge came from the Roman Catholic Church. In mathematics, physics, astronomy, and medicine, new ideas were proposed, all of which could be quickly spread by the printing press. Scientists began to criticize existing theories and make their own observations.

The belief that the earth was the center of the universe was challenged by Nicolaus Copernicus in 1543, and his ideas were supported by Galileo Galilei in the next century. Both men thought that the sun was the center of the solar system, although few people believed them, but the explanation of how the earth revolves daily on its axis around the sun was not made until 1687, when Isaac Newton described the force of gravity that holds the solar system together.

This explanation would not have been possible without the advances made in mathematics. New measuring instruments, such as the thermometer and the barometer, were invented. So too was the microscope, used by Anton van Leeuwenhoek to magnify animal and plant cells. In medicine, Andreas Vesalius illustrated the anatomy of the human body, and William Harvey, who first discovered the circulation of blood, showed how the body worked.

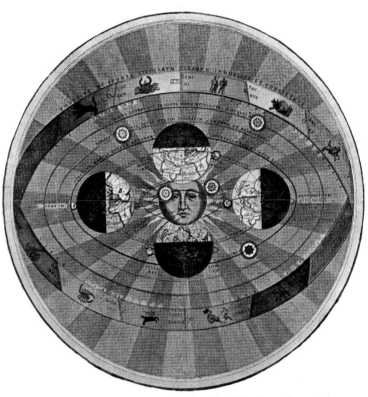

▲ The solar system as described by Nicolaus Copernicus, a Polish scientist, in 1543. The sun is shown at the center of the solar system with the earth orbiting around it.

▼ Louis XIV visits the Académie Royale des Sciences in 1671. Founded in 1666, the French Académie was a learned body that helped spread new ideas.

▲ Isaac Newton, the scientist who explained the force of gravity. He also invented a reflecting telescope and introduced a branch of mathematics called calculus.

France, the absolute state

During the 1600s and 1700s much of Europe was ruled by kings, queens, and emperors who were extremely powerful. Unlike European royal families today, these rulers were directly responsible for the economic, political, and social lives of their countries.

Louis XIV, ruler of France from 1643 to 1715, was the most powerful of these **absolute monarchs**. All decisions were approved by him, and power was concentrated in his hands; he once summed up his position in the words *"L'état, c'est moi"*: I am the state. His absolute control was admired and copied by other European monarchs.

After a series of rebellions between 1648 and 1653 by leading nobles against the crown, France welcomed the strong rule of its king. But Louis required money for his many adventurous schemes. This money was raised by increasing taxes and exploiting the wealth of France's colonies in Canada and the West Indies. The first great canal to be built in Europe since Roman times was constructed, and new roads and financial grants all helped to build up industry and commerce.

The wealth created was used to make the French army into the biggest in Europe and to finance the wars that Louis fought. After his death, however, further costly wars drained the country's resources and left France in a weakened condition.

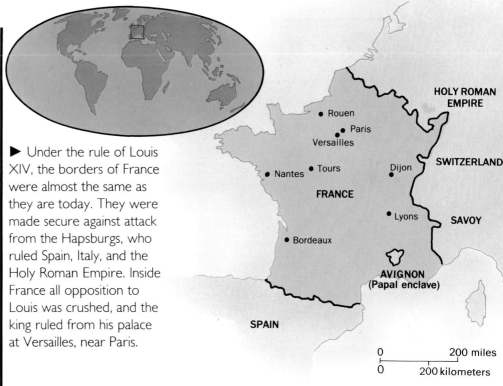

▶ Under the rule of Louis XIV, the borders of France were almost the same as they are today. They were made secure against attack from the Hapsburgs, who ruled Spain, Italy, and the Holy Roman Empire. Inside France all opposition to Louis was crushed, and the king ruled from his palace at Versailles, near Paris.

◀ Louis XIV was the dominant ruler in Europe throughout the 1600s. He believed in absolutism—that the king has complete control to rule his country as he wishes.

▼ At the salon of Madame Geoffrin in 1725. Groups of aristocrats met regularly to discuss art and philosophy. These salons were the only places that women could have any impact on the intellectual or political life of the day.

▼ The royal palace at Versailles was designed to glorify Louis XIV, the "Sun King." Surrounded by vast gardens and a park, the huge palace contained a Hall of Mirrors and many other sumptuously decorated state rooms. The high cost of running the palace was met by imposing taxes on the impoverished population.

▼ Plague, famine, and high taxes made many of the poor people homeless, and they were forced to beg for food. The French peasants relied on the annual harvest—if the harvest failed they went hungry. Lack of food also made them more vulnerable to catching diseases such as the plague.

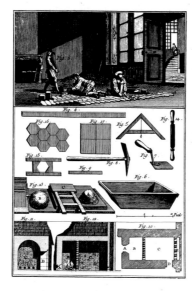

The Enlightenment

In almost every country in western Europe in the middle of the 1600s, an intellectual movement grew up, which became known as the Enlightenment or the Age of Reason. It questioned existing beliefs and attempted to "throw light" on every area of human activity and thought. Its participants believed in the power of people to reason things out for themselves. Their thirst for knowledge included an interest in science and a curiosity about the peoples, plants, and animals from those parts of the world the Europeans were only just discovering for themselves.

One of the main achievements was the vast encyclopedia (*left*) of all human knowledge, compiled between 1751 and 1777 by the French **philosopher** Denis Diderot. Another Frenchman, René Descartes, provided the philosophical basis of the movement with the saying: "I think, therefore I am."

This new thinking challenged the existing authorities, such as the Church: some scientists, such as Galileo, were imprisoned, and the books of Descartes were banned. But this questioning of authority could not be suppressed and in France was one of the causes of the **French Revolution**.

The emergence of Russia

Before 1450, much of southern Russia was controlled by the Empire of the Golden Horde, a powerful state ruled by the Mongols of central Asia, who managed to isolate Russia from European developments. But as the power of the Mongols lessened, the small region of Muscovy exerted its independence. In 1480, its ruler, Ivan III, declared himself "**Czar** of all the Russias" and appointed himself protector of the Orthodox Church.

Ivan III rebuilt Moscow with the help of Italian architects and began to expand the Muscovite state westward. Expansion continued under successive czars, and by 1647 Russia dominated Siberia in the east but was unable to expand any farther toward Europe because of Polish and Swedish power.

In 1682 Peter the Great became Czar of Russia, and until his death in 1725, he attempted to create a strong, **westernized** state. He toured western Europe in 1697 and 1698, and on his return to Russia he introduced many reforms to modernize his country, giving it new industries and an improved education system.

After a lengthy war with Sweden, which ended in 1721, Russia gained control of the Baltic Sea. A new capital city — St. Petersburg (Leningrad) — was built on the Baltic, which finally established Russia's presence in the West as a political power.

KREMELIN

▲ The Palm Sunday parade in what is now Red Square in Moscow. The city is clustered around the triangular fortress in the center, called the Kremlin. St. Basil's Cathedral (*on the left*) was built in the 1550s to celebrate the victories of Ivan IV.

◀ Peter the Great in carpenter's dress. He traveled around Europe and learned shipbuilding techniques, which he later used to create a powerful Russian navy.

▼ Although the grand buildings of Russian cities were built of stone, the houses and churches of the Russian peasants were usually constructed with wooden logs.

1648–1760

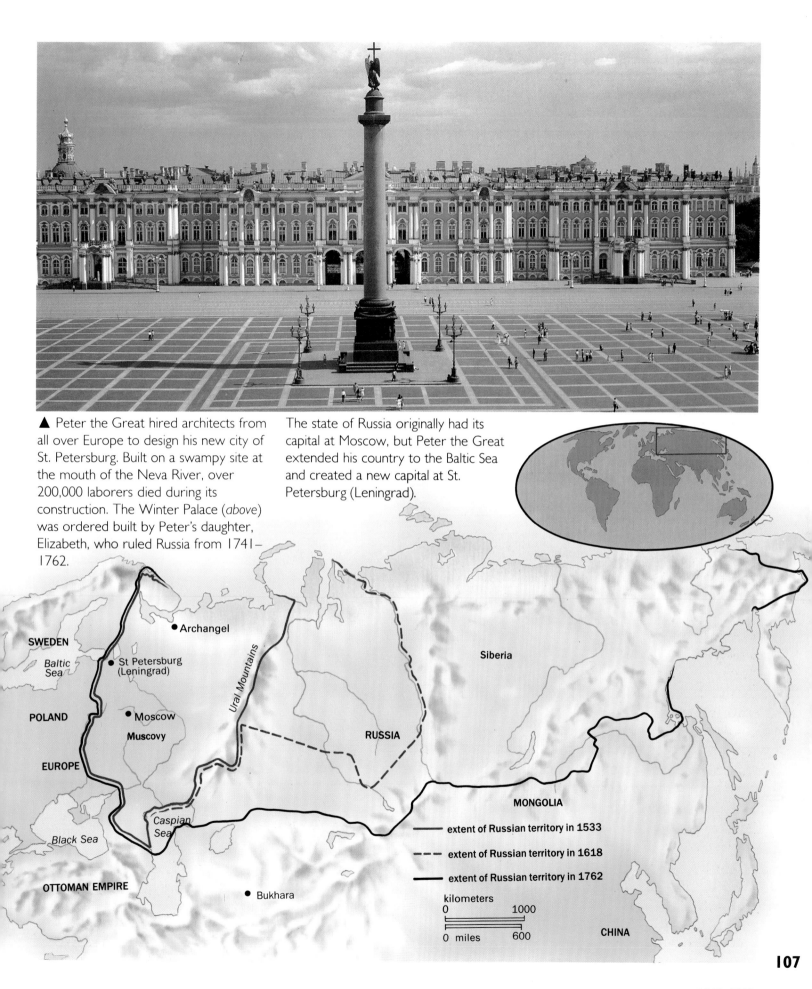

▲ Peter the Great hired architects from all over Europe to design his new city of St. Petersburg. Built on a swampy site at the mouth of the Neva River, over 200,000 laborers died during its construction. The Winter Palace (*above*) was ordered built by Peter's daughter, Elizabeth, who ruled Russia from 1741–1762.

The state of Russia originally had its capital at Moscow, but Peter the Great extended his country to the Baltic Sea and created a new capital at St. Petersburg (Leningrad).

SWEDEN

Baltic Sea

POLAND

EUROPE

Black Sea

OTTOMAN EMPIRE

• Archangel

• St Petersburg (Leningrad)

• Moscow

Muscovy

Ural Mountains

Caspian Sea

• Bukhara

Siberia

RUSSIA

MONGOLIA

—— extent of Russian territory in 1533

------ extent of Russian territory in 1618

——— extent of Russian territory in 1762

kilometers
0   1000

0 miles   600

CHINA

China

From 1368 to 1644 the Ming dynasty ruled China. At first the Ming emperors brought order and stability to the vast country, whose growing population was twice that of all Europe. But harvest failures and high taxes caused discontent and weakened the Empire, which was also being threatened by attacks from Japan and by the Manchus, a highly organized tribe from Manchuria in the northeast.

In 1644 the Manchus invaded China and seized power, setting up a new imperial dynasty—the Ch'ing dynasty. They strengthened the state and expanded it north into Mongolia and west into Tibet and Sinkiang. They established trading links with Europe and exported porcelain, silk, cotton, and tea. However, the Chinese imported only gold and silver from Europe and continued to develop their own culture, so that by 1750, China was wealthy, secure, and quite independent of Europe.

Japan

During the 1400s and 1500s Japan was torn apart by civil war. But in 1603 peace was restored when one of the many warlords—Ieyasu Tokugawa—became the new **shogun**, or military leader, under the emperor. Like China, Japan developed independently of the outside world. From 1639, all Christian missionaries were expelled, trade with Europe all but stopped, and the Japanese were forbidden to go abroad.

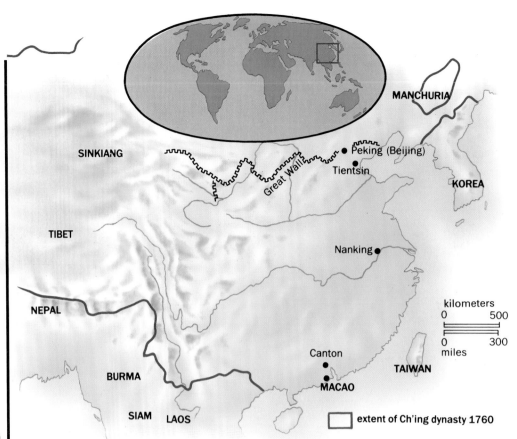

Both Ming blue-and-white ware (*right*), hand made at the imperial factory, and the more basic pots and vases, manufactured in numerous small workshops all over China, were produced for the home market and for export to Europe. The "china" was carefully packed before it was shipped (below).

1648–1760

▲ Weaving silk on a loom. The Chinese silk industry was a vast enterprise, employing many thousands of workers, especially women, to produce silk textiles for home use and for export to Europe.

▲ Although the emperor ruled Japan in name, real military and administrative power lay with the shogun. The shogun Ieyasu Tokugawa brought peace to Japan in 1603 and united the country under his family's rule until 1867.

▶ After 1639 the only port in Japan open to foreigners was at Nagasaki, where the Dutch, Chinese and Koreans were allowed to trade.

▼ The elaborate ritual of dressing a *samurai*. The *samurai* were the aristocratic warrior class in Japan, famed for their bravery and devotion to the emperor. At one time they had the right to kill any commoner who offended them.

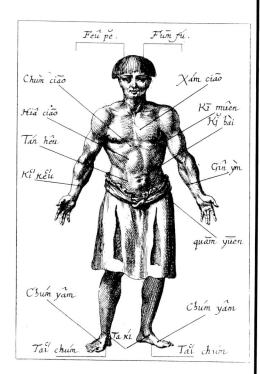

▲ Acupuncture—in which a number of fine needles are inserted into the skin to relieve pain and treat various ailments— has only recently been used in Western medicine, yet has been common practice in China for centuries.

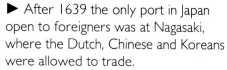

Australia and New Zealand

By 1700 Europeans had penetrated every part of the world. They had established trading links across the Atlantic and Pacific oceans and had completely disrupted **indigenous** societies in the Americas, Southeast Asia, and parts of Africa. Australia was the last "unknown continent" that the Europeans invaded.

Both the Aborigines in Australia and the Maoris in New Zealand had developed thriving societies based on a nomadic existence of hunting and fishing which had remained undisturbed by any contact with the outside world. This way of life came to an end with the arrival of the Europeans. In 1605 Dutch explorer Willem Jansz became the first European to arrive in Australia; in 1642 Abel Tasman sailed around the continent—without ever seeing it!

Australia remained undisturbed until 1768, when the British Admiralty sent Captain James Cook to explore the continent. He made three voyages in all, claiming Australia for the British crown in 1770 and exploring the whole of the western Pacific. In 1788 the first Europeans settled in Australia — convicts transported from Britain to serve their sentences. These colonists soon overcame the powerless Aborigines. In 1840 a British settlement was established in New Zealand, and the Maoris were forced to accept the rule of the British.

▲ One of the crew from Captain Cook's ship the *Endeavour* barters with a Maori in New Zealand for a crawfish.

▲ When he reached Australia, Captain Cook found many birds, animals, and plants previously unknown in Europe. One of the animals was the kangaroo.

Dutchman Abel Tasman set out in 1642 to find the fabled southern continent. He sailed around Australia without ever sighting it, but he discovered Tasmania, named after him, and New Zealand, which was named after the Dutch province of Zeeland.

▶ The Maoris came to New Zealand from the Pacific Islands in about A.D. 800, traditionally in seven canoes. By the 1700s they numbered about 100,000 people. This European drawing shows the son of a Maori chief, Otegoongoon, with his face "curiously tattooed."

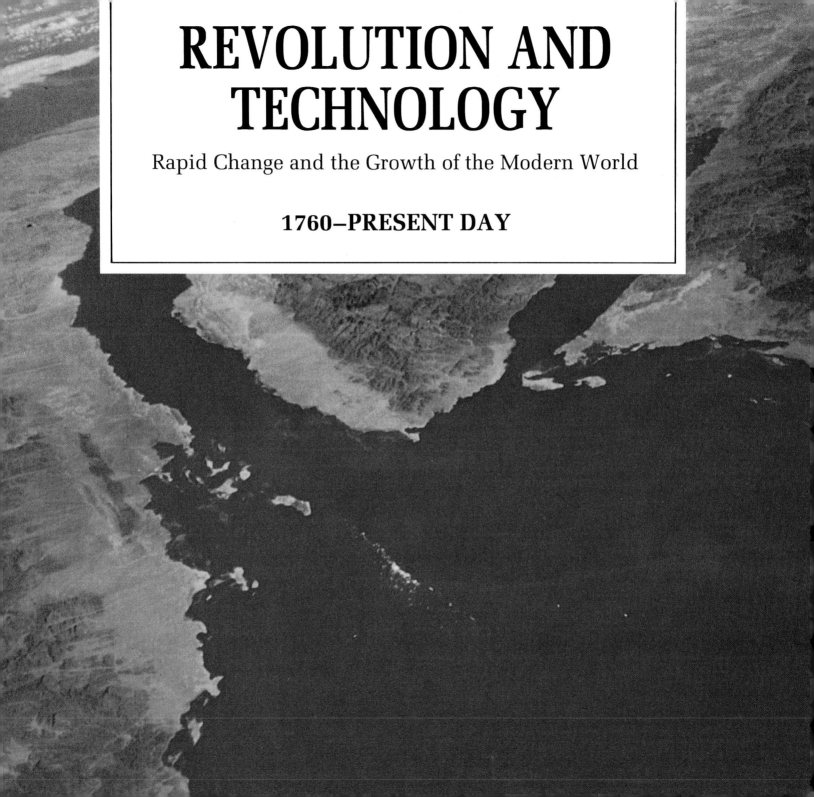

REVOLUTION AND TECHNOLOGY

Rapid Change and the Growth of the Modern World

1760–PRESENT DAY

the Atlantic Ocean to the Caribbean in 1492, European merchants and sailors had been exploring the world. They had founded colonies and established trading links in every part of the world.

By 1760 Britain was the most powerful colonial and trading power in the world. Britain ruled large empires in North America and India. The British navy dominated the seas, and Britain had established an extensive overseas trading network. France too was a wealthy and powerful **nation**, with colonies in the Caribbean. Spain and Portugal governed most of Central and South America and, like the Netherlands, had colonies and trading posts in Africa and the Far East. In Asia, the Russians governed a huge empire that stretched from eastern Europe to the Pacific Ocean, and the Ottoman Turks ruled over much of eastern Europe, the Middle East, and North Africa.

However, most of Africa and the wealthy empires of China and Japan remained independent of European control, although China and Japan had limited trade with Europe.

▶ In 1760 there were few parts of the world that were not under European control. North and South America, the coast of Africa, India, and much of the Far East were governed from Europe, and from them merchants sent back valuable cargoes, which made Europe the wealthiest part of the world.

(*page 113, bottom left*) A British merchant ship known as an East Indiaman, in Calcutta, India.

(*page 113, bottom right*) A drawing showing ambassadors at the Meridian Gate in Beijing (Peking), China. There were four cities at Beijing, each surrounded by great walls. China was prepared to have limited trade with Europe—through the port of Canton only.

The 13 Colonies

ATLAN

CARIBBEAN SEA

Spanish possessions

PACIFIC OCEAN

Portug posses

◀ In many parts of the world the European rulers enslaved the local population and made them work on sugar, tea, and other plantations.

112

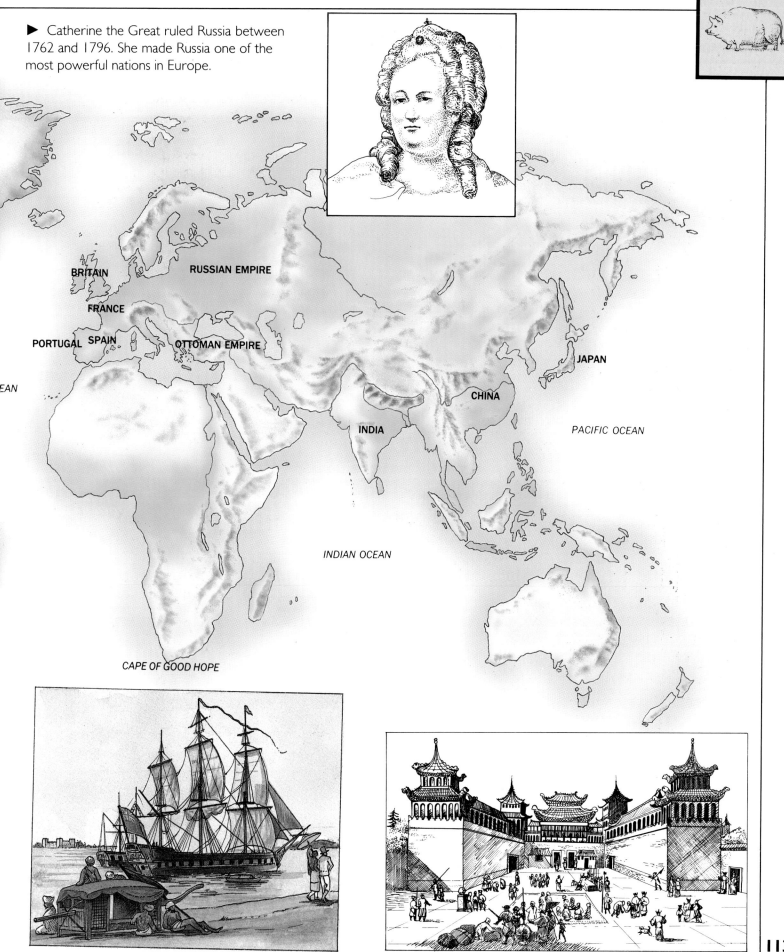

► Catherine the Great ruled Russia between 1762 and 1796. She made Russia one of the most powerful nations in Europe.

BRITAIN

RUSSIAN EMPIRE

FRANCE

PORTUGAL SPAIN

OTTOMAN EMPIRE

JAPAN

CHINA

INDIA

PACIFIC OCEAN

INDIAN OCEAN

CAPE OF GOOD HOPE

113

The Industrial Revolution

During the 1700s Europe experienced a number of important social and economic changes whose effects remain today. The population doubled, and people began to move from the countryside to the cities. By 1800 Paris and London each contained more than one million inhabitants, and other European cities were growing fast. To feed this rising population, new agricultural techniques were developed.

The biggest changes took place in industry, where Britain, followed by other countries, underwent what is known as the Industrial Revolution. Starting in Britain in about 1760, the Industrial Revolution transformed the way in which goods were produced. Machinery was developed that was powered by coal and water. Inventions such as the steam engine and steam pump, the blast furnace, and the spinning jenny revolutionized the manufacture of goods, particularly textiles (yarn, cloth, etc.). Methods of working changed too. Previously, most textiles had been produced in people's homes in "cottage industries." Now new machines were operated in factories where many workers—men, women, and children—labored together under one roof.

As a result, British manufacturers could produce more goods than their foreign competitors. By 1815 Britain led world trade and was "the workshop of the world."

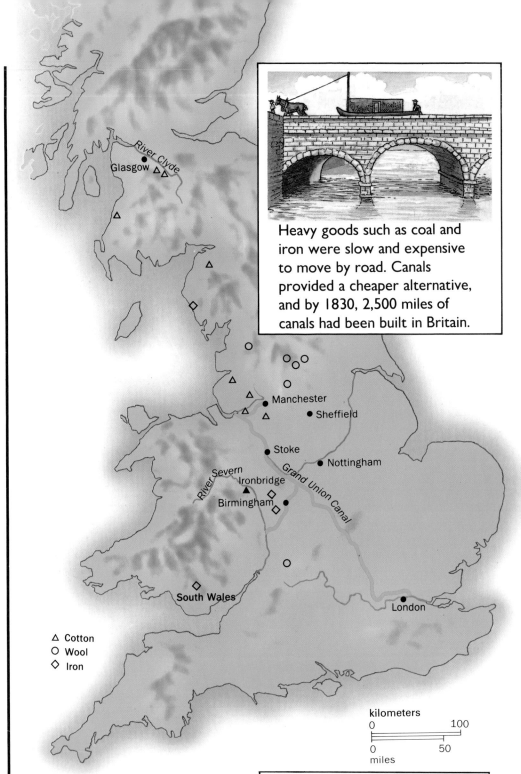

Heavy goods such as coal and iron were slow and expensive to move by road. Canals provided a cheaper alternative, and by 1830, 2,500 miles of canals had been built in Britain.

△ Cotton
○ Wool
◇ Iron

kilometers
0 ———— 100
0 ———— 50
miles

▲ After 1760 Britain became the industrial center of the world. The country possessed plentiful supplies of coal and iron ore. A large network of roads, navigable rivers, and canals was created to transport these raw materials to new industrial towns. In the towns they were made into manufactured goods, notably textiles and ironware, and exported around the world.

The Agricultural Revolution

During the early 1700s an agricultural revolution began in Britain. Farmers developed new methods of farming, including more efficient crop rotations, and new equipment. These improvements increased food production, but fewer workers were needed, so families were driven off the land into towns.

1760-1815

► Water power had been used for centuries to drive machines, and so the first factories of the Industrial Revolution were all situated near a supply of running water, usually in hilly areas. After 1768 the development of the coal-fired steam engine meant that factories could be built wherever there was a good supply of coal.

▼ The British engineer Thomas Newcomen built the first steam engine in 1712, but it was only used for land drainage. In 1768 James Watt improved the original design and adapted it to drive factory machines.

▼ During the Agricultural Revolution, farmers began to experiment with new breeds of pig and other livestock. Larger pigs, such as this Berkshire hog, and new breeds of sheep produced twice as much meat as before. Improved milk yields from cows led to an increase in dairy products.

◄ In 1764 James Hargreaves invented the spinning jenny—a machine that could spin up to 100 threads of cotton at one time. Previously, cotton was spun by hand, one thread at a time, by workers in their homes. The jenny replaced this domestic industry with workers who were employed in factories.

► The development of factories was seen as a threat to the jobs and independence of craftworkers. From 1811 to 1813 a group of workers known as Luddites rioted, smashing textile machinery in protest of their new working conditions. This cartoon shows the Luddite leader disguised as a woman.

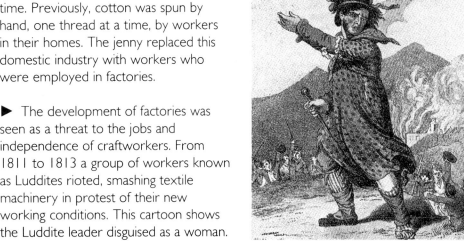

The American Revolution

Toward the end of the 1700s two revolutions occurred: the first in North America and the second in France. In both of them, people demanded democratic government and rights for the individual.

In 1763 Britain had defeated France to become the major colonial power in North America. But after the war, relations between Britain and its 13 colonies on the North Atlantic coast began to deteriorate. The immediate cause of these problems was taxation. The colonists made their own local laws, but their finances and trade were controlled by the British government. Increasingly, the colonists resented paying taxes to a government that they did not elect or choose, and in which they were not represented.

In 1774 representatives from the 13 states came together in a Continental Congress to discuss relations with Britain. But revolution broke out in 1775 when shots were exchanged between colonists and the British army at Lexington, Massachusetts. In 1776 the Continental Congress declared the 13 colonies **independent** of Britain, and in 1781 the American forces defeated the British army. In 1783 the British recognized the independence of their former colonies. The rebels had won, and they set up a new, united nation—the United States of America. In 1789 George Washington became the first president of the new nation.

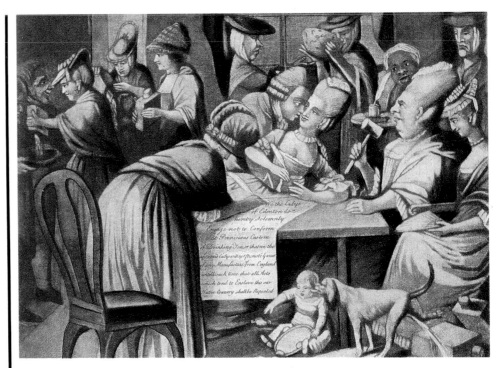

▼ Signing the Declaration of Independence, issued in 1776 by the Second Continental Congress. Drawn up by Thomas Jefferson, the document declared that "all men are created equal" and that they have the right to "Life, Liberty and the pursuit of Happiness." Ideas such as these had a strong influence on later revolutionary movements.

▲ In 1773 a group of women in Edenton, North Carolina, protested against a British tax on tea by refusing to drink tea. That same year, colonists in Boston threw cases of tea into the harbor in a similar protest, now known as the Boston Tea Party.

The French Revolution

By 1789 French society was already deeply divided, for the middle classes resented the power of the king, the aristocracy, and the Church. The people were heavily taxed, and many of them were starving. In 1789 King Louis XVI summoned the French parliament to raise more taxes. Almost immediately, the **bourgeoisie**, the middle-class representatives, challenged the power of the king and set up the National Assembly to rule France. Riots broke out, and the people of Paris stormed the royal fortress of the Bastille. The revolution then quickly spread throughout the country. In 1792 the National Convention, which had replaced the Assembly, deposed the king and declared France a republic. Power passed to a political group known as the Girondists. In 1793 they executed the king for treason. Later the same year, a more radical group of politicians known as the Jacobins took power under Maximilien Robespierre. This "Reign of Terror" lasted until 1794, during which they executed all those suspected of opposing the revolution. In 1799 the revolution ended when Napoleon seized power.

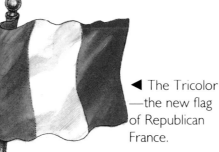

◄ The Tricolor —the new flag of Republican France.

Areas of resistance

Paris

Nantes

La Vendée FRANCE

Bordeaux

Lyons

Marseilles

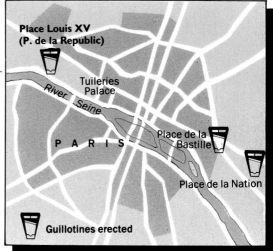

Place Louis XV (P. de la Republic)

Tuileries Palace

River Seine

P A R I S

Place de la Bastille

Place de la Nation

Guillotines erected

▲ The French Revolution began in Paris when the citizens stormed the Bastille fortress in 1789. But it soon spread to the rest of the country. Some areas stayed loyal to the king; in the Vendée region of western France, a royalist revolt in 1793 was put down with considerable ferocity.

▼ Women led many of the marches and demonstrations during the French Revolution, demanding greater freedom and enough food to feed their families. Many suffered from starvation during the bad harvests. Despite their part in the revolution, women were never allowed to vote or participate in the government.

▲ The guillotine quickly became the symbol of the revolution. It was used to execute aristocrats and other opponents of the revolution. More than 40,000 men and women were guillotined between 1789 and 1794.

Napoleonic Europe

The American colonies won their independence from Britain in 1783, with considerable French support. France had wanted revenge for the loss of its American colonies to Britain in 1763. But the American Revolution inspired people in France to seek their own freedom, and in 1789 a revolution broke out in France itself (see page 117).

By 1793 all of Europe was involved in the French Revolution. An alliance of European states was formed against France, but France had an army of more than 750,000 —the biggest in Europe—and by 1797 France had defeated all its enemies except Britain. This success was due to the quality of the French commanders, particularly Napoleon Bonaparte, who in 1796, at the age of 26, had taken command of the army. In 1799 he seized control of the French government, and in 1804 he crowned himself emperor of the French.

Napoleon reorganized the law, administration, education, and economy of France. His army was unbeatable, and by 1812 he had conquered most of Europe. But his attempts to conquer Spain met with great resistance. In 1812 he unsuccessfully invaded Russia, and his army suffered heavy losses retreating from Moscow. In 1815 Napoleon was defeated by the British and their allies at Waterloo, Belgium. He was sent into exile on the South Atlantic island of St. Helena, where he died in 1821.

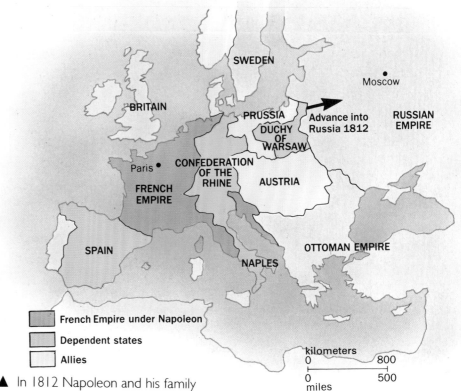

French Empire under Napoleon

Dependent states

Allies

▲ In 1812 Napoleon and his family ruled an empire that dominated Europe. He reorganized Germany and Italy into allied states, and Prussia and Austria were considerably reduced in size and power. Only Britain remained independent. But the French Empire was weakened by the wars against Spain and Russia and was finally overthrown in 1815.

▶ Napoleon was a military genius who had conquered most of Europe by 1812. His empire did not survive him, but many of his administrative and educational reforms are still in force in France today.

◀ A plate from a dinner service made for Napoleon. In 1798 Napoleon led a French army to Egypt to cut British trade links with India. While in Egypt, French archaeologists excavated the ancient Sphinx, which had been buried in the desert sand for hundreds of years, and investigated the pyramids.

◀ In 1808 Napoleon invaded Spain and placed his brother Joseph on the throne. Although the French introduced many reforms, their rule was not popular, and the Spanish people revolted. Many civilians were killed, as this painting by Francisco Goya shows.

▼ The dates of independence of the European colonies in South America.

MEXICO
1821

CENTRAL AMERICAN
FEDERATION
1821-1838

VENEZUELA
1830

British, Dutch, and French colonies
in GUYANA

COLOMBIA
1819

ECUADOR
1830

PERU
1821

BRAZIL 1822

BOLIVIA
1825

PARAGUAY
1811

CHILE
1818

URUGUAY 1828

ARGENTINA
1810

kilometers
0   1000

0   500
miles

▲ The French controlled the Caribbean island of Haiti, the richest colony in the world. Its wealth was created by the many slaves who worked on its plantations. In 1801 the slaves, led by Toussaint l'Ouverture, rose in revolt. L'Ouverture was captured and killed by the French in 1803, but in 1804 Haiti became an independent country.

▼ José de San Martín (left), liberator of Argentina and Chile. He led his army across the Andes Mountains, a military achievement.

▲ The Spanish colonies in South America refused to accept the rule of Joseph Bonaparte and declared their independence from Spain. Led by Simón Bolívar (above) and José de San Martín, all the Spanish territories became independent by 1825.

119

The Impact of Revolution

Industrial nations

The upheavals caused by the Industrial and French revolutions affected every aspect of social and political life for the next 100 years.

Although the Industrial Revolution began in Britain, the new **technologies** and methods of production soon spread to Belgium, France, Germany, and Italy. At first, Britain was strong enough to fight off any competition. In 1850 one fourth of all the world's trade passed through British ports, and over one third of the world's industrial output was British. The first railroad was tested in northern England in 1825, and the first passenger train operated between Liverpool and Manchester in 1830. The railroad revolutionized communications, and by 1870 there were 15,500 miles of railroad track in Britain alone.

Other countries soon began to challenge British industrial and economic supremacy. After 1870 new steel and chemical industries were established in Germany, and by 1900 the United States had become the most powerful industrial nation in the world, with vast steel, oil, and food production industries. Russia, too, developed an iron and steel industry, and Japan started to build up an industrial economy.

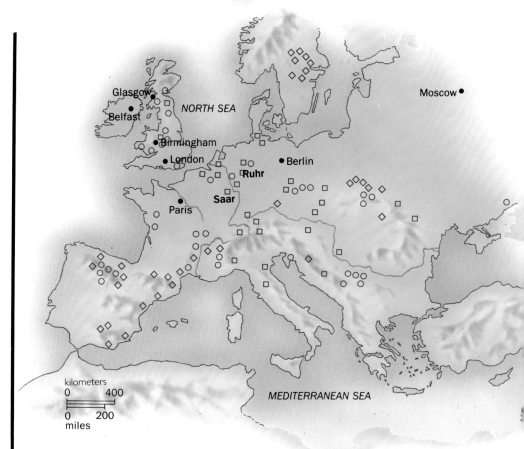

○ **Coalfields**
◇ **Iron ore fields**
□ **Textile industry**

▲ The Industrial Revolution began in Britain but soon spread throughout Europe. Mines and factories opened up near supplies of coal and iron, and new towns were built to accommodate the expanding work force. Across Europe, the population increased dramatically due to advances in medical technology.

▶ Men, women, and children worked long hours for low pay in the mines and factories of industrial Britain. In the early coal mines, men hacked the coal out of the seams, and women then dragged it or carried it along the narrow tunnels. Starting in the 1830s, however, laws were introduced to improve working conditions.

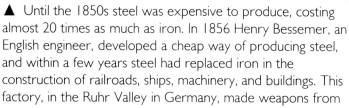

▲ Until the 1850s steel was expensive to produce, costing almost 20 times as much as iron. In 1856 Henry Bessemer, an English engineer, developed a cheap way of producing steel, and within a few years steel had replaced iron in the construction of railroads, ships, machinery, and buildings. This factory, in the Ruhr Valley in Germany, made weapons from steel.

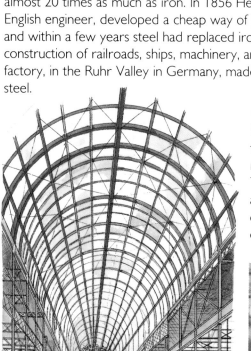

◄ In 1851 Britain held an international exhibition in London to show off the industrial and manufacturing might of the country. The Great Exhibition was housed in a remarkable iron and glass building called the Crystal Palace; it was erected in only a few months.

▲ The Industrial Revolution created many new towns and enlarged many old ones, but conditions in the towns were overcrowded and poor. Many of the houses were badly built and had no running water or sewage disposal, and they quickly became slums. Disease and poverty were common in all major cities.

► Poor children were sent to work in factories or even mines as soon as they were old enough to walk and talk. They received little formal education and were made to work long hours for little pay. Child labor was common in European and American factories until well into the 20th century.

Europe after 1815

After Napoleon's defeat in 1815 the victorious allies met in Vienna to redraw the map of Europe. The French monarchy was restored, and Austria became dominant in central Europe. Throughout Europe, aristocratic government was restored, and Napoleon's reforms were reversed everywhere except in France.

The Vienna settlement lasted only a few years. The French Revolution had introduced to Europe two ideas: democracy, in which the state belonged to the people and not the king, and **nationalism**, in which people speaking a common language and living together in one country or region had the right to rule themselves. However, the 1815 settlement left many peoples under undemocratic, foreign control, and major uprisings soon occurred. In 1821 the Greeks revolted against their Turkish rulers and won independence in 1829, and in 1830 the Belgians overthrew Dutch rule.

In 1848 revolutions occurred throughout Europe. The monarchy was again overthrown in France, and nationalists revolted against Austrian rule in Italy, Germany, and Hungary. By 1851 the revolts had been crushed. But nationalism was strong in Italy and Germany. Led by Count Camillo Cavour, the Italian states drove out the Austrians by 1866, and Italy was united by 1870. In 1871 Germany was united under Prussian rule.

▲ In Britain, the Chartists—a mass movement of workers—demanded political reform and the right for all men to vote. Between 1838 and 1848 they held vast demonstrations and presented a series of petitions to Parliament.

▶ In 1848 the German thinker Karl Marx wrote the *Communist Manifesto,* urging workers to overthrow undemocratic governments. At the time, the book was not widely read, but during the 20th century, Marx's ideas have strongly influenced modern revolutionary movements in Russia, China, and South America.

▼ In 1848 many countries in Europe erupted in revolution.

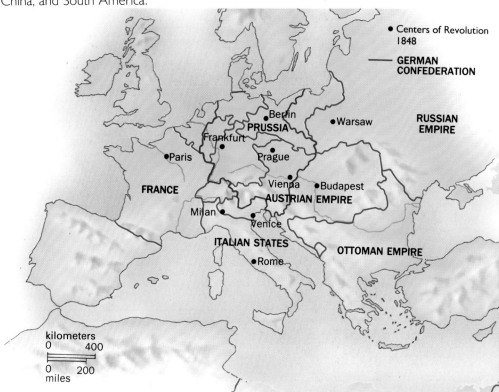

1815–1880

Science

▲ This contemporary cartoon attacks the British biologist Charles Darwin, who, in 1859, published *The Origin of Species*. In this book he proposed that over many thousands of years humans had evolved from apes.

▼ In 1861 the French chemist Louis Pasteur discovered that diseases do not occur by themselves but are the result of germs. This discovery led him to develop pasteurization, a method of sterilizing (cleaning) milk.

▲ A picture taken during the American Civil War, one of the first wars to be recorded by photograph. In 1839 the Frenchman Louis Daguerre produced the first successful photograph. Only one photograph could be produced at a time.

Throughout the 1800s, there was a constant stream of new technological developments. Science and medicine were revolutionized, as a series of remarkable developments transformed the way in which people lived and thought about the world around them. Scientists such as Louis Pasteur discovered the cause of diseases; doctors such as Joseph Lister introduced effective antiseptics for the prevention of infections; and, for the first time, the workings of the human mind were scientifically investigated when the Austrian doctor, Sigmund Freud, began his investigations into mental illness at the end of the century. In 1859, the British biologist Charles Darwin shocked the Western world when he suggested that human life had begun, not with their creation by God, but through a long process of evolution from the apes.

▲ In the 1890s, the Frenchwoman Marie Curie investigated uranium, which is now used to produce nuclear power.

▲ In the late 1800s and early 1900s, the Austrian Sigmund Freud studied human behavior by interpreting dreams.

The growth of the United States

When the United States became independent from Britain in 1783, it consisted of only the 13 original British colonies on the Atlantic east coast. But the colonies grew quickly after independence, and in little more than 80 years the U.S. had tripled in size, reaching right across to the Pacific Ocean and up to the Arctic Circle in the north.

In 1803 France sold the land to the west of the Mississippi River for $15 million, which doubled the size of the country. By 1867 gains from Spain, Britain, Mexico, and Russia gave the country its present shape. But throughout the 1800s there were fierce battles for control between the European settlers and the Native Americans, or American Indians, who had lived there for thousands of years. Though brave, the Indians had little defense against troops, and by 1890 they had been overcome and confined to reservations.

Between 1803 and 1900, the population of the United States rose from four million to 90 million. Many of these people were immigrants fleeing from poverty and oppression in Europe. They spoke many different languages and brought many skills to their new country. Some prospered, others remained poor, but a rich and strong nation emerged. By 1900 the United States was the world's most powerful industrial and commercial nation.

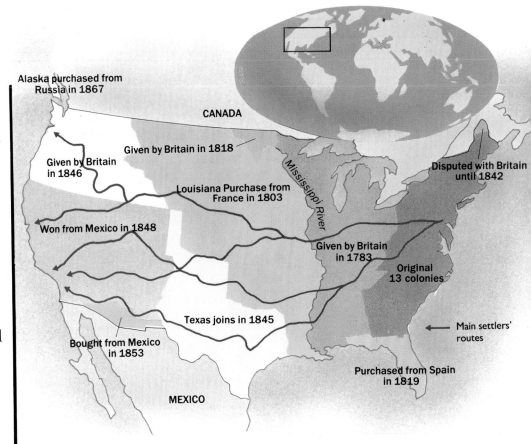

▲ By 1848 the original 13 American colonies on the Atlantic coast had expanded across the continent to the Pacific Ocean. It was many years before these vast tracts of land were fully settled by farmers and their families, who moved slowly westward from the crowded eastern states.

▼ In 1831 the first steam-powered railroad was opened in the U.S., and by 1869 the first transcontinental railroad was completed, with a total of 52,000 miles of track. The railroad did much to open up the West and to create a truly united country. The advertisement below dates from 1882.

◀ The early North American settlers lived hard lives. Many could not live peacefully with the local Indians, and they were always at the mercy of bad weather or harvest failure. The settlers built homes of turf or soil, and it was years before they could afford to build secure wooden houses.

▼ In 1861 civil war broke out in the U.S. between the Southern states, who wished to keep slaves on their plantations, and the Northern states, who wished to abolish **slavery**. The Northern states won the war in 1865, and the South was devastated. This picture shows a New York ferry converted into a gunboat for use by the Northern states.

▶ Sitting Bull was chief of the Sioux tribe and one of the most famous of Indian leaders. In 1876, after refusing to go to a reservation, he masterminded the Battle of the Little Bighorn, in which General George Armstrong Custer and all his soldiers were killed. Sitting Bull fought for the rights of the Indian peoples until his death in 1890.

▶ Harriet Tubman was an escaped slave who spent much of her life fighting slavery. During the Civil War she helped organize an escape network known as the Underground Railroad, through which thousands of slaves escaped to freedom. Tubman herself led more than 300 slaves to freedom through the Underground Railroad.

Imperialism and Empire

Empire builders

In 1880 most of Africa consisted of independent nations—their economies were based on agriculture, and they traded with other African countries. Contact with Europe was limited, though the British, French, and Portuguese maintained small colonial trading posts on the coast, and the Ottoman Empire had loose control of northeastern Africa. By 1914, with the exception of the independent states of Ethiopia and Liberia, every part of Africa was controlled by Europeans. Africa's economy had been transformed to provide raw materials for European industries.

Similarly, the British had established complete control of India and its neighbors, and of Australia and New Zealand; much of the Far East was ruled by other European powers. The main reason for this expansion overseas was that by 1880 the Industrial Revolution had spread across Europe. The new industries needed cheap supplies of raw materials, and this led European nations to exploit the vast and untapped resources of Africa and the Far East. By 1914 Britain had built up the world's biggest empire. It covered one fourth of the world's land surface and included one fourth of its population. France, Belgium, Portugal, Spain, Italy, and the

continued on page 128

1880

Portuguese
British
French

1914

LIBERIA
ETHIOPIA

Spanish
German
Italian
Belgian
Independent

▲ In 1880 most of Africa consisted of independent nations, with only the Ottoman Empire ruling any significant territory in Africa. By 1914 the continent had been carved up by Europeans and only two nations remained independent of foreign control.

▲ The Englishwoman Mary Kingsley was an enterprising explorer who traveled throughout West Africa in the late 1800s. Many of the people she encountered had never met a European woman before.

▼ Cecil Rhodes was prime minister of the British-controlled Cape Colony in South Africa. He dreamed of building a railroad from the Cape in the south to Cairo in the north that would run entirely through British territory.

1880–1914

▲ In 1869 the Suez Canal was opened, connecting the Mediterranean Sea to the Indian Ocean. Because of its strategic position on the route from Britain to its empire in India, it was acquired by Britain in 1875.

▲ British influence in India was considerable. Many of the British people living in India preserved as much as possible their British customs and ways of life. Here two Englishmen take afternoon tea, attended by their Indian servants.

▼ Southern Africa is rich in gold and diamonds. During the late 1800s a number of powerful mining companies were set up, controlled by Europeans and using slave labor.

European settlement of South Africa

The first European settlers in South Africa were the Dutch, who established a colony on the Cape of Good Hope in 1652. The British took over the colony in 1814 and in 1833 abolished the slavery of black Africans on the farms and plantations. This angered the Boers, as the original Dutch settlers were known, and in 1835 they began their Great Trek inland to form two new independent republics.
Continual conflicts between the Boers and the British led to war in 1899. By 1902 the British had won, and in 1910 the country was united and became an independent state known as the Union of South Africa.

newly united Germany all established colonies in Africa. Meanwhile the United States acquired territory in the Caribbean and the Far East. By 1914 the United States and eight European nations controlled 85 percent of the world's land surface.

China and Japan

Until the mid-1800s very few Europeans had been allowed into the empires of China or Japan. The Chinese in particular had a hatred of foreigners and allowed them to trade only in certain areas. Britain, however, was eager to extend its influence. In 1839 it went to war with China, and in 1842 the Chinese were forced to sign a treaty surrendering Hong Kong and allowing Britain to trade in other ports. Within China, revolts against the Ch'ing dynasty weakened the Empire, allowing European influence to increase. The Chinese government's failure to resist the Europeans in turn led to further rebellions, and in 1911 a revolution finally overthrew the Empire and established a republic.

Japan had almost no trading contact with foreigners until 1853, when an American naval squadron sailed to Japan and forced the Japanese to trade with the United States. Europeans followed, and Japan made trade agreements with many countries. Over the years, Japan developed railroads and factories and by 1905 was beginning to become a major industrial nation.

▲ By 1905 Britain, France, and Russia dominated much of China, and Japan had gained an empire of its own in Korea and Taiwan.

► From 1898 to 1900 a Chinese secret society known as the Boxers rebelled against Western intervention, attacking railroads, factories, and European embassies. The rebellion was finally put down by European, Russian, and Japanese armies, who established control over much of the country. This Chinese cartoon attacks Westerners.

▼ In the 1850s the waterfront of the Chinese city of Canton was full of Europeans, but they were not allowed into the interior of China for many years.

▲ In 1853 and 1854 the American naval commander Matthew Perry visited Japan and forced the government to grant trading concessions to American shipping. It was the first Japanese contact with foreigners in over 200 years.

▲ In 1872 the first railroad was completed in Japan by British engineers. Within 30 years, more than 5,000 miles of track had been laid, and Japan had become one of the most powerful industrial countries in the world.

▼ In their rush to modernize their country, many Japanese people, including the royal family, gave up their traditional costumes in favor of Western clothes.

129

A changing world

In the years immediately after 1900 wars broke out in Europe, Africa, and the Far East, and there was internal unrest in many industrial nations. Much of the trouble was caused by the fact that the European powers were competing against each other to control trade and to enlarge their empires. By 1900 Germany had become the major industrial power in Europe, and this led to considerable rivalry with other established industrial nations such as Britain. An **arms race** developed between the European powers. Britain, France, and Russia formed an alliance to protect themselves against Germany, and Germany allied itself with Austria.

There was also considerable social unrest in many countries. In 1905 revolution broke out in Russia against the autocratic rule of the Czar. Although unsuccessful, the revolution seriously weakened the country. In 1912 war broke out in Eastern Europe as the local peoples fought to overthrow their Turkish rulers and prevent Austria from divided into two heavily armed camps. In Ireland there was almost civil war by 1914, caused by the demands of the Irish for self-government. Throughout Europe poor wages and bad working conditions led to much social unrest; by 1914 the whole continent was in turmoil.

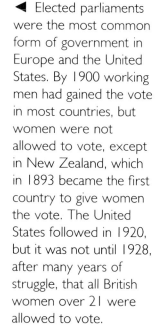

◄ Elected parliaments were the most common form of government in Europe and the United States. By 1900 working men had gained the vote in most countries, but women were not allowed to vote, except in New Zealand, which in 1893 became the first country to give women the vote. The United States followed in 1920, but it was not until 1928, after many years of struggle, that all British women over 21 were allowed to vote.

▼ A dole line in Britain. During the late 1800s governments began to take responsibility for the welfare of their people. Many countries introduced compulsory education, and pensions were provided for the old. State insurance was introduced to protect workers against unemployment or sickness, and workers received "dole" money if they lost their jobs.

▼ In the years leading up to 1914 there was an arms race in Europe between the major powers. Weapons such as this German howitzer were capable of great destruction.

Transportation

In the 1800s new forms of transportation revolutionized communications throughout the world. Railroads, steamships, automobiles, bicycles, and, in the early years of the 1900s, airships and aircraft all increased the speed and efficiency of human travel. An organized tourist industry started to develop, and people began to visit foreign countries in large numbers. Trade between different countries became easier and cheaper, and refrigeration enabled perishable foodstuffs to be transported around the world. As a result of these developments, all parts of the world were linked together as never before.

▼ The development of the bicycle in the mid-1800s offered a cheap form of transportation and recreation to many people.

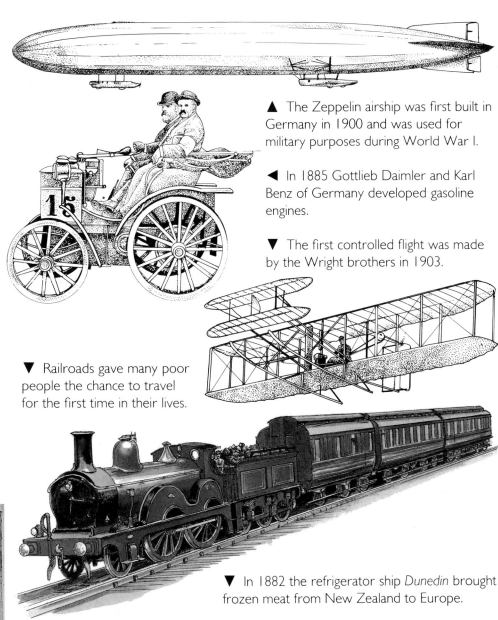

▲ The Zeppelin airship was first built in Germany in 1900 and was used for military purposes during World War I.

◄ In 1885 Gottlieb Daimler and Karl Benz of Germany developed gasoline engines.

▼ The first controlled flight was made by the Wright brothers in 1903.

▼ Railroads gave many poor people the chance to travel for the first time in their lives.

▼ In 1882 the refrigerator ship *Dunedin* brought frozen meat from New Zealand to Europe.

The World at War

World War I

In 1914 war broke out in Europe, lasting four years and involving the whole world. The immediate cause of the war was the assassination of the heir to the Austrian throne in June 1914. Austria blamed its neighbor and enemy Serbia for the murder and declared war on it; soon all of Europe was at war. Few nations remained neutral, and the fighting extended overseas for control of Germany's African and Far Eastern colonies, and for Turkish territories in the Middle East.

Between France and Germany a line of defensive trenches stretched along the Western Front, where millions of soldiers were killed. In Eastern Europe, the war was equally savage. For three years there was a stalemate, but in 1917 the Russian Revolution forced Russia to leave the war. In an effort to starve Britain and France into surrender, Germany attacked their supply ships in the Atlantic. Some American ships were sunk, and in 1917 the United States declared war on Germany. The vast numbers of American troops proved decisive, and in November 1918 the war ended. Of the 65 million men who fought in the war, 10 million died, and more than 20 million were injured. It was the bloodiest war in human history.

▲ Most soldiers in **World War** I spent their time in damp and dangerous trenches on the Western Front being bombarded by enemy shells.

► For the first time in history, whole populations were involved in war. Many women worked, producing armaments and keeping industry going while the men were in the army.

▼ World War I split Europe into two armed camps.

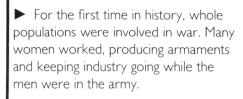

1914–1945

The Russian Revolution

In 1917 a revolution took place in Russia that was to change the course of modern history. The revolution occurred because many people suffered poverty and hardship. The government of Nicholas II was brutal and inefficient, and it fought the war against Germany very incompetently.

In March 1917 a **general strike** broke out in Petrograd (as St. Petersburg [now called Leningrad] was then known) in protest against the conduct of the war and the economic chaos at home. The army joined the strike and Nicholas was forced to abdicate (give up) his throne. A provisional government was formed but it had little support, and in November 1917 the Communists (or Bolsheviks, as they were known) seized power. Led by V. I. Lenin, the Bolsheviks

Vladimir Ilyich Ulyanov (Lenin)

quickly took control of the country and declared a Soviet republic, known today as the Soviet Union. The Bolsheviks made peace with Germany. Large estates were broken up and given to the peasants, banks were taken into state control, and workers were given control of their factories. The world's first communist state had been founded.

► In 1924 Joseph Stalin succeeded Lenin as head of the Soviet Union. He took all the land into state ownership and forced the peasants to work on the new collective farms. This is a poster advertising collectivism.

◄ Alexandra Kollontai was the only woman in the Bolshevik government. She was committed to economic change and to equality between women and men.

▲ Before the revolution four fifths of the Russian population were peasants. Some of them found work hauling barges down the Volga River.

133

The aftermath of war

In 1919 representatives from 32 nations met at Versailles, France, to draw up a peace settlement. Four empires — Germany, Austria, Russia, and Turkey — had collapsed, and many countries wanted independence. The map of Europe was redrawn, and some new countries such as Poland and Czechoslovakia came into existence. The League of Nations was set up to work for peaceful settlements rather than war.

The Versailles settlement was soon in trouble. The German economy collapsed because of the reparations (payments) Germany was forced to make for its part in the war. Other nations suffered from the heavy repayments they had to make to the United States for money borrowed during the war. The result was considerable political and economic upheaval. In 1929 an economic crisis known as the Great Depression began.

Millions of people were thrown out of work. During the 1930s there was widespread unemployment and social unrest in Europe and in the United States. The president of the United States, Franklin Roosevelt, helped the poor and unemployed through a program of government aid known as the New Deal. In Germany, however, an extreme nationalist, Adolf Hitler, came to power in 1933. He promised to set unemployed Germans to work by restoring German power in Europe.

▶ The Treaty of Versailles in 1919 broke up the German, Austrian, and Russian empires and replaced them with new states throughout Eastern Europe. Germany became smaller and was split into two parts. Poland and Finland re-emerged as independent nations. The Austro-Hungarian Empire was split into four new countries, with parts of it also going to Italy, Poland, and Rumania. Three new states were created on the Baltic.

This is the great picture upon which the famous comedian has worked a whole year.

6 reels of Joy.

Charles Chaplin
IN
"THE KID"

Written and directed by Charles Chaplin
A First National ⓝ Attraction

◀ During the early 1900s, the first movies appeared. They were in black and white and had no sound. By 1930, they were in color and had sound. Many movies were produced in Hollywood, the movie capital of the world.

▼ A scene in Wall Street in 1929, as the value of shares on the American Stock Exchange crashed and investors lost confidence in the U.S. economy. Banks failed and an economic depression began that soon spread throughout the world.

▲ India remained a British colony after 1919. But demands for independence grew, led by the Indian nationalist Mohandas Karamchand Gandhi (second from left).

▼ In 1936 civil war broke out in Spain between the Republican government and the Fascists led by General Francisco Franco. Helped by Italy and Germany, Franco defeated the government in a brutal war. He ruled Spain as **dictator** from 1939 to 1975. In this poster a soldier off to fight the Fascists tells his child: "I go to fight for your future."

▲ The Depression caused terrible suffering to American farmers. Prices fell and drought affected the crops. Whole families were forced to leave their farms in the Midwest to look for other work in California.

▼ **Fascism** was carried to extremes by Hitler, leader of the Nazi party, who was named German chancellor in 1933. Economic, cultural, and religious life were all brought under central government control. Here Hitler leads a military parade in honor of his birthday in 1941.

Voy a luchar por tu porvenir

World War II

When Hitler became the leader of Germany in 1933, he created a German empire in Central Europe. By 1939 he had seized Austria and Czechoslovakia. Most European nations were anxious to avoid the horrors of another war, but when in 1939 Hitler invaded Poland, Britain and France declared war on Germany. Italy joined the war on the German side.

For six years, war raged in Europe, North Africa, Russia, and the Pacific. Continual air raids destroyed many cities. By 1941 Germany had conquered most of Europe, except for Britain, and had advanced into Russia. In the Far East, Japan allied with Germany and invaded China, Burma, and other parts of Southeast Asia.

In December 1941 Japanese planes bombed the U.S. naval base at Pearl Harbor, Hawaii. The United States sided with Britain, and together they reconquered North Africa, invaded Italy, and in 1944 liberated France from German control. As American and British troops advanced on Germany from the west, Russian troops advanced from the east. As they neared Berlin in April 1945, Hitler committed suicide, and the war in Europe ended. In August the Americans dropped atomic bombs on the Japanese cities of Hiroshima and Nagasaki, and Japan surrendered. It was a brutal end to a brutal war. Fifty million people had been killed and another 43 million wounded. Europe was devastated.

▲ War touched every part of the globe as soldiers from all over the British Empire fought the war on Britain's side.

▲ One of Hitler's most dreadful aims was to destroy the entire Jewish population of Europe. More than six million Jews and other peoples died in concentration camps such as this one at Buchenwald, Germany.

▼ In 1942 the German conquest of Europe reached its greatest extent. Very few countries managed to avoid the fighting.

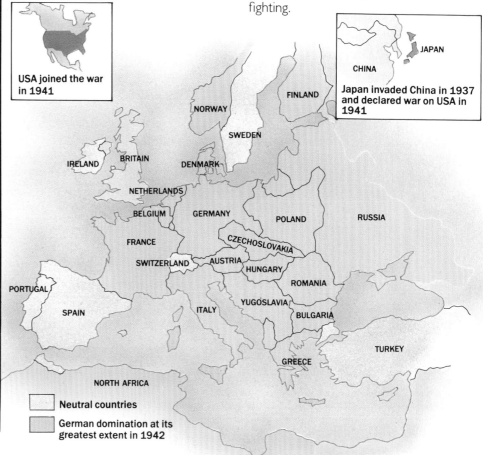

USA joined the war in 1941

Japan invaded China in 1937 and declared war on USA in 1941

Neutral countries

German domination at its greatest extent in 1942

136

▲ On August 6, 1945, an atomic bomb was dropped on the Japanese city of Hiroshima. This photograph shows the terrible devastation caused by the bomb.

◄ In 1945 the American, Russian, and British leaders—Franklin Roosevelt, Joseph Stalin, and Winston Churchill—met at Yalta in Russia to decide how to divide up postwar Europe.

▼ After 1945 the German capital Berlin, like Germany itself, was divided. Conflicts arose, and in 1961 the Berlin Wall was built to divide East Berlin from West. In November 1989, protests in East Germany led to the dismantling of the wall, and Germany was reunified.

▲ On August 15, 1947, India gained independence from Britain. India became mainly Hindu, and a new state, Pakistan, was created for the Muslims. Both Burma and Ceylon (Sri Lanka) also received their freedom. There was considerable bloodshed during this partition of India, and the Indian leader Gandhi was assassinated in 1948.

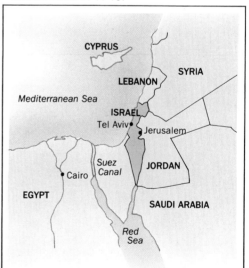

In 1947 a Jewish homeland was created in Israel. In 1948 the Palestinian occupants of the country were defeated by the new Israeli army. Since then, three more wars have broken out between Israel and its Arab neighbors.

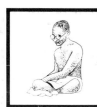

A Troubled World

The Cold War

In 1945 American troops liberated Western Europe from German control, and Russian troops had liberated Eastern Europe. Together the **superpowers** of the Soviet Union and the United States dominated Europe. But differences soon emerged between them. The Soviet Union felt threatened by the American presence in Europe, and the United States feared that the Soviet Union wanted to extend its control of Eastern Europe. By 1949 Europe was divided into two armed camps, both engaged in what was known as the **Cold War**.

When war broke out in Korea in 1950 and then in Vietnam in 1957, the Soviet Union and China supported one side, and the United States supported the other. In other disputes too, in the Middle East, Africa, and South America, the two superpowers supported opposing sides. The years after 1945 were also marked by an increasing nuclear arms race between the superpowers.

In 1985 Mikhail Gorbachev became Soviet premier and introduced a new policy of *glasnost* (openness) and *perestroika* (economic reform) in the Soviet Union. Rivalry between the two powers decreased as both the United States and the Soviet Union discussed the possibility of

continued on page 140

▲ By 1949 Europe was divided into two armed camps: the North Atlantic Treaty Organization (NATO) and the Warsaw Pact.

▶ In 1962 the two superpowers came close to war when it was discovered that the Soviet Union had placed nuclear missiles on the island of Cuba, only 90 miles from the American mainland. This cartoon shows Nikita Khrushchev, the Russian leader, and John Kennedy, the American president, wrestling on top of nuclear weapons.

◀ Students confront Soviet troops in 1968 when Czechoslovakia tried to break away from Soviet control. But by 1989 Soviet control had relaxed and popular pro-democracy movements swept through Czechoslovakia, Hungary, Rumania, and the rest of Eastern Europe.

1945–

◀ Superpower rivalry extended into outer space. In 1957 the Soviet Union launched the world's first satellite into orbit around the earth. In 1961 the Soviet Union became the first country to put a human into space. The United States launched a series of rockets with the aim of landing people on the moon. This they achieved in 1969. In 1975, however, both countries worked together on a joint space mission.

▶ In 1969 the American astronaut Neil Armstrong (*right*) became the first person to walk on the moon. For the first time in human history, it was possible to see our planet Earth from space (*far right*).

▼ Vietnamese refugees run to a helicopter that will take them to safety. Between 1957 and 1975 war raged between North and South Vietnam. The Soviet Union and China supported the North, and the United States supported the South. The war cost many American and Vietnamese lives, and ended with victory for the North after the U.S. withdrew its troops in 1973.

▲ In 1987 Ronald Reagan, the American president, and Mikhail Gorbachev, the Soviet leader, signed a treaty to dismantle intermediate-range nuclear missiles. This decision was welcomed by many people who hoped that the treaty marked the first step toward complete nuclear disarmament.

139

nuclear disarmament. In 1989 popular uprisings in Eastern Europe also eased tension. In 1991 the Soviet Union and the U.S. became allies once again in the Gulf War.

China

In 1912, China became a republic after a revolt by the Kuomintang political party overthrew the Manchu emperor (Manchurians had ruled China since 1644). However, the new government had no real control; the powerful **warlords** ruled the many provinces of China. In 1926 the Kuomintang general Chiang Kai-shek defeated the warlords with the help of the Chinese Communist Party. He set up a national government in the city of Nanking. Once in power, he threw the Communists out of the government and killed many of their leaders. Fighting broke out between the two sides. By 1949 the Communists, led by Mao Tse-tung, were triumphant.

The Communists under Mao began rebuilding China. They put industry and agriculture under state control China allied itself with the Soviet Union and received technical aid in developing the country. But in 1960 the two governments quarreled, and the aid stopped. Since then, the Communist Party has kept the country under tight control. Dissent against the government was squashed during the Cultural Revolution between 1966 and 1969.

◀ In October 1934 the Communists decided to leave their stronghold on the coast of China and move inland. Led by Mao Tse-tung, 100,000 people set out on the Long March. They covered 40 to 70 miles a day and arrived at their destination a year later. Only 30,000 of the original marchers completed the 6,000-mile march.

▲ In order to unite the country, the Chinese leader Mao Tse-tung encouraged a "cult of personality." Millions of people bought and read *The Thoughts of Chairman Mao*, his collection of sayings.

▶ In 1989 students in Beijing (Peking) and other cities requested more democracy and freedom in China. The Chinese government refused to grant these requests and crushed the peaceful student movement with military force. Many people were killed or imprisoned.

1945–

Technology and Pop Culture

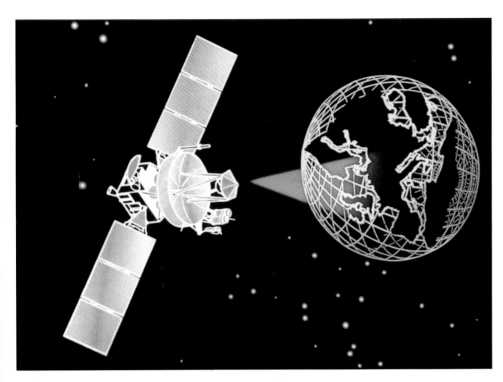

Today the regions of our world are more closely linked than ever before. It is possible to travel around the globe in hours, and satellites can broadcast events and relay messages around the globe in seconds. Television has brought every area of the world into our homes, and there are few places in the world left undisturbed by tourists. As a result, differences between the various countries of the world are slowly breaking down.

Computers speak their own common language to each other across the globe. Fashions in clothes, music, design, and art are now universal.

▲ The first satellite was launched by the Soviet Union in 1957. Since then, thousands of satellites have been sent into orbit around the earth.

◄ Satellite communication has brought television to the remotest parts of the world.

Pop music started in the 1950s. Groups such as the Beatles (*left*) and singers like Michael Jackson (*right*) are known in every country. Their records sell millions of copies.

A divided world

Since 1945 a wide gap has emerged between the rich countries of Europe, North America, Australasia, and the Far East and the poorer countries of Africa, Asia, and Central and South America.

The rich countries all have highly developed industries and economies. In Western Europe, 12 countries have joined together in a Common Market to bring their economies closer together, and in the Far East, Japan has become one of the richest nations in the world. In contrast, many of the poor countries have little industry and only primitive agriculture. Many of these countries only received their independence in the 1960s and 1970s when the European powers such as France and Britain began to dismantle their overseas empires. In countries such as Tanzania and Zambia, this move to independence was peaceful, but in Algeria and Mozambique, for example, there was much bloodshed. Some of these new nations are prosperous, but many suffer considerable poverty, made worse by famine, civil war, disease, and overpopulation.

In order to build up their economies, many poor nations have borrowed money from the rich nations of Europe and the United States. The repayment of these loans has been expensive and has kept many of the poor nations in poverty. Today the gap between rich and poor is one of the world's most urgent problems.

▲ The conflict between Israel and its Arab neighbors has made the Middle East one of the world's most troubled areas.

◀ In 1910 South Africa became an independent nation. Since then the minority white population has held absolute power through a system called **apartheid** (racial segregation). Apartheid denies all rights to the majority of South Africans, who are black. In 1990 the ban against political opposition groups was lifted, and some political prisoners, such as Nelson Mandela of the African National Congress, were freed after many years in prison. In 1991 President F. W. de Klerk introduced legislation to repeal the remaining apartheid laws.

▼ In 1979 Ayatollah Khomeini became the leader of Iran. He ruled the country according to the Koran, the Islamic holy book. Until his death in 1989, he was the leader of a revival of Islamic fundamentalism.

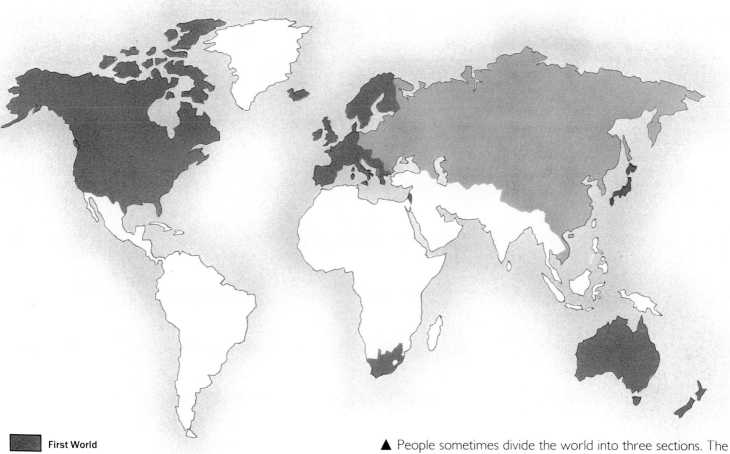

First World

Second World

Third World

▲ People sometimes divide the world into three sections. The so-called First World, or "developed market economies," contains the United States and its allies in Western Europe, the Far East, and Australasia. The Second World, or "centrally planned economies," consists of the Soviet Union, China, and other communist states in Eastern Europe and Asia. The **Third World**, or "developing market economies," includes most of Africa, Asia, and South and Central America. However, many people dislike these labels because they are artificial and are based on economic wealth rather than the culture of the countries and have been imposed by the richer countries on to the poorer ones.

▼ Many parts of Africa have suffered crop failures, drought, floods and cyclones. In some countries, such as Mozambique (below), civil wars have led to the collapse of the national economy and food production. Such countries have become dependent for aid on Western countries.

▼ Some of the countries in Central America have been in a state of political unrest. Troops leave a Sandinista helicopter in Nicaragua.

143

One world?

Over the last 200 years, the population of the world has risen—from about 600 million to more than 5 billion (5,000 million) in 1990. Some experts believe that by the year 2000 it will have risen to 8 or 10 billion. Of this huge population, two thirds live in the Third World, in areas where poverty is so great that one in five children die before they reach their fifth birthday, and most families lack decent food, housing, and medical attention.

Poverty is not the only problem facing the world today. During the 1980s scientists have become more aware that human actions are harming our planet Earth. Industrial pollution and the exploitation of the world's natural resources are destroying irreplaceable plant and animal life and harming the delicate structure of the atmosphere. Disasters such as the industrial accident at Bhopal, India, in which at least 2,500 people were killed by poisonous gas in 1984, have alerted people to the dangers of our modern world.

We are now more aware than ever that what happens in one part of the world has a direct effect on the rest of the world. This awareness has led to the formation of groups like Friends of the Earth and Greenpeace, whose aims are to protect the people, animals, and plant life of our planet and ensure that future generations will be able to enjoy the world we live in today.

144

▲ Clearing the rainforest for the trans-American highway. Since World War II over half of the world's rainforest has been cut down, destroying thousands of species of plants and animals.

▼ In 1984 famine broke out in Ethiopia. Irish singer Bob Geldof arranged a huge international rock concert, called Live Aid. The Live Aid project raised money to send food and other supplies to Ethiopia, as well as technical expertise to help the Ethiopians prevent another famine.

▶ Children in Oman learning about the wildlife of their country. All over the world people are becoming more aware of the need to conserve the earth's natural resources.

Glossary

Words in this book in **bold** are explained in the glossary below.

Absolute monarch A ruler such as Louis XIV who was completely responsible for governing a country.

Agriculture The science of raising animals and growing crops.

Alliance A friendly agreement between peoples, groups, or countries.

Ambassador A person representing the interests of one country in another country.

Amphitheater An oval or circular open-air theater with seats around a central space.

Anthropology The scientific study of human beings.

Apartheid The policy of racial segregation pursued in South Africa.

Aqueduct A bridge built to carry water.

Arable land Land that is plowed for growing crops.

Archaeology The study of ancient buildings, tools, and other remains of a culture.

Aristocracy The nobility or other privileged groups in a country.

Armada (means "fleet of warships") Usually describing the Spanish Armada, which in 1588 sailed against England.

Arms race Rivalry between countries to build up supplies of weapons and weaponry.

Aryan The name given to the Indo-European invaders of India.

Astrolabe An instrument for measuring the height of the stars above sea level. It was used by early navigators and sailors.

Authoritarian Expecting total obedience.

Balance of power A situation when two or more nations are equal in power.

Bantu (means "people") A group of people from central and southern Africa who speak one of the Bantu languages.

Barbarians A term used by the Romans to describe the nomadic invaders of their empire.

Baron A powerful landowner whose lands were given to him by the king.

Bourgeoisie The name given in Europe to the middle class.

Bronze An alloy (mixture) of copper and tin.

Caliph Religious ruler of a Muslim country.

Capitalism An economic system in which goods are produced for profit, and investment is provided by a small group of people.

Caribs The original Indian peoples of the Caribbean.

Caste A group of people within the Hindu religion considered to have the same social status or class.

Citadel An elevated fortress protecting a city.

Citizen A person who lives in a town or city.

City-state A city that is also an independent country.

Civilization A developed and settled way of life including living in towns or cities.

Civil war A war between different groups of people within one country.

Claimant A person who has a claim to the throne.

Cold War Hostility between two countries that does not result in actual fighting.

Colony A settlement abroad that is ruled or governed by another country. Colonists are people who leave their home country to live in a colony.

Commerce Trade or buying or selling.

Common land A large piece of land that can be used by anyone.

Communism An economic and political system in which the state owns all property and means of production.

Conquistador (means "conqueror") The name given to the Spanish adventurers who sailed to South America in search of gold and riches.

Consul One of the two ancient Roman officials elected each year.

Crusade Military expedition launched from Europe to recover the Holy Land from Muslim rule.

Culture Art, literature, music, and painting. Culture is also used to describe the way of life of the people of a country or region.

Czar A Russian word meaning "emperor" used to describe the rulers of Russia before 1917.

Democracy A country in which the government is chosen by the people.

Dictator An unelected head of state who rules a country by force.

Dynasty A ruling family or series of rulers from one family.

Economy The financial and business affairs of a country.

Empire A group of countries under one ruler.

Excommunicate To expel someone from the Church.

Fascism A political system in which all power is concentrated in a strong, centralized state led by a dictator.

Feudal system A system of government based on land ownership and allegiance to the lord of the manor, the baron, or the king.

Fossils Remains of ancient plants or animals, preserved as stone.

French Revolution The revolution in France against the royal family (1789–95).

General strike A refusal to work by employees in every trade in one country until certain demands are met.

Glacials Periods when large areas of earth were covered by ice; ice ages.

Guild An association of workers sharing the same skill who join together to protect their interests and train new members.

Hapsburgs The ruling house of Austria from the 1200s to the early 1900s.

Hieroglyphics Writing using picture symbols called hieroglyphs.

Hominid A member of the family *Hominidae*, which includes modern humans and their ancestors.

Immunity The body's natural defense against disease.

Independence Self-government for a colony.

Indigenous A word used to describe the native peoples, plants, and animals of a country.

Interglacials The warmer periods between glacials.

Irrigation A method of supplying dry land with water so that crops can grow.

Islam The religion of the Arabs and other peoples who worship Allah and follow Muhammad as his prophet. Followers of Islam are known as Muslims.

Junk Chinese sailing boat used to transport goods.

Kiln A furnace used for firing pottery.

Kingdom A country ruled by a king or queen.

Land bridge A strip of land connecting two larger areas of land.

Maize A type of corn.

Maroons Fugitive slaves living in the West Indies.

Merchant economy This term is used to describe an economy based on trade.

Mesoamerica A term for Mexico and Central America.

Minuscule Writing developed by scholars working for Charlemagne around 800.

Missionary A religious person who goes to another country to convert people to his or her own religion.

Monarchy A country ruled by a king or queen.

Mosaic A picture made up of numerous pieces of different colored stone or glass set in a wall, floor, or ceiling.

Nation A group of people under one government.

Nationalism Determination of a group of people to run their own affairs as a state or nation.

Neanderthals A group of early people who lived in Europe and parts of Africa and Asia from about 100,000 B.C. to 35,000 B.C.

Netherlands The name given to the kingdom of Holland.

New World A term used by the Europeans to describe the Americas.

Nomads People who move with their herds or flocks of animals in search of grazing land.

Oracle The means of consulting the gods about the future, or asking for advice.

Pastoralists People who herd and graze flocks of animals.

Pasture Land covered with grass used for grazing cattle or sheep.

Patron A wealthy supporter, usually of the arts.

Pharaoh (means "great house") The title of the king of ancient Egypt.

Philosophy The study of the meaning of existence.

Pilgrim A person who journeys to a religious site to worship there.

Plantation A large estate or area of land planted with trees or one crop such as sugar beets, tea, tobacco, or cotton.

Pope Head of the Catholic Church, based in Rome.

Primates A group of animals that includes humans and monkeys.

Pueblo Town or village built by Native Americans.

Renaissance (means "rebirth") A period of European history from the 1400s to the 1600s when people rediscovered the learning and work of the ancient Greeks and Romans.

Republic A country with an elected government but no royal family.

Revolution A total, sometimes violent, change of political or economic conditions and their replacement with a new system.

Saga A long story concerning legendary or historical figures and events, passed down by word of mouth from parent to child.

Satrapies Administrative areas in ancient Persia.

Seals Cylinders engraved with a device which leaves an impression on soft wax.

Semitic languages The group of languages that includes modern Arabic, Aramaic, and Hebrew.

Senate (Roman) A group of aristocrats in Rome who advised the consuls, or later the emperor.

Shogun Military ruler of Japan before the mid-1800s.

Silk Road The main land route between China and Europe. Camel trains walked along it carrying travelers and goods for trade.

Slavery The ownership of people as property.

Smelting The process of extracting metal by heating ore to a high temperature.

Socialism A political system based on the belief that the people as a whole should own and control a country's wealth.

Spice Islands The islands of Southeast Asia from where spices were exported to Europe.

State A country or part of a country which governs its own affairs.

Steppes The grassy plains of central Asia.

Superpower A nation that has power and influence throughout the world, based on its economic and military might.

Tax Money paid by people to a government for the administration of the country.

Technology The practical use of scientific discoveries and inventions.

Terra-cotta Unglazed, usually brownish-red pottery.

Third World A term sometimes used to describe developing market economies, in particular the poor countries of Africa, Asia, and South and Central America.

Tournament A mock battle to test the strength and skills of knights and prepare them for warfare.

Trade The process of buying and selling goods.

Treaty A written agreement between one or more countries.

Triangular trade The sea trade in slaves and goods in the 1600s and 1700s.

Tribe A group of people often descended from the same person or sharing the same language and culture.

Tropics The areas of land around the equator.

Villein A peasant tied to the land and under the authority of the lord of the manor.

Vizier In ancient Egypt the title of a chief minister or the governor of a province.

Warlord A military leader who governs a part of a country as if it is his own property.

Westernized A word used to describe countries or ways of life that have been influenced by the Western part of the world such as the United States or Europe.

World War A war fought between nations throughout the world.

Ziggurat A temple tower built as a pyramid in ancient Babylonia.

Europe	**Near East**	**Africa**

Europe

B.C.

*c.***33,000** Neanderthals die out.

*c.***20,000** Cave art flourishes in France and Spain.

*c.*10,000 End of last ice age.

*c.***2000** Minoans build Knossos in Crete.

*c.***1600** Beginning of Mycenaean civilization in Greece.

*c.***1450** Destruction of Minoan civilization.

*c.***1100** Phoenician supremacy in the Mediterranean.

900–750 Rise of city-states in Greece.

776 First Olympic Games.

753 Founding of Rome (traditional date).

480 Greeks defeat Persian invasion.

*c.***400** Athens rises to power in Greece.

431–404 War between Athens and Sparta.

*c.***300** Rome rises to power in Italy.

264–146 Punic wars between Rome and Carthage.

27 Octavian becomes first Roman emperor.

A.D.

330 City of Constantinople (Istanbul) founded.

370 Huns from Asia invade Europe.

395 Roman Empire divided in two.

Near East

B.C.

*c.***8000** First farming in Mesopotamia.

*c.***7000** Walls of Jericho built.

*c.***3500** Beginnings of Sumerian civilization.

*c.***3200** First writing in Sumeria.

2360 Akkadian Empire founded by Sargon.

1792–1750 Rule of Hammurabi, king of Babylon.

*c.***1500** Iron first smelted by the Hittites.

*c.***1200** Beginnings of Jewish religion.

*c.***1200** Israelites colonize Palestine.

*c.***721–705** Assyrian Empire at height of its power.

586 Babylonian captivity of Jews.

*c.***500** Persian Empire at its height.

334 Alexander the Great begins conquest of Persia.

A.D.

*c.***30** Crucifixion of Jesus Christ.

70 Romans destroy Jerusalem; *diaspora* (dispersal) of Jews begins.

132 Jewish rebellion against Rome.

226–651 Sassanians rule Persian Empire.

330 Capital of Roman Empire transferred to Constantinople (Istanbul).

Africa

B.C.

*c.***40,000** Earliest specimens of modern humans (*Homo sapiens*) found in Africa.

*c.***5000** Farming introduced into northern Africa.

*c.***3200** First dynasty in Egypt.

*c.***2800** Pyramids of Giza begun.

*c.***2686** Beginning of "Old Kingdom" in Egypt.

*c.***2500** Sahara begins to dry out.

*c.***1570** Beginning of "New Kingdom" in Egypt.

*c.***900** Kingdom of Kush becomes independent of Egypt.

*c.***900** Nok culture of Nigeria begins.

814 Phoenicians found colony at Carthage.

*c.***600** Iron smelting developed in northern Africa.

*c.***600** Bantu people move into southern Africa.

*c.***550** Arabs from Yemen colonize Ethiopia.

332 Alexander the Great conquers Egypt.

30 Egypt becomes a Roman province.

A.D.

350 Kingdom of Axum (Ethiopia) conquers Kush.

350 Christianity reaches Ethiopia.

429–535 Vandal Kingdom in northern Africa.

**Asia and the Far East**	**The Americas**	**Australasia**
B.C. *c.*6000 Rice cultivated in Thailand. *c.*2500–1500 Indus Valley civilization. 1766 Shang dynasty begins rule in China. 1122 Chou dynasty begins rule in China. *c.*650 Introduction of iron-working. *c.*563 Birth of the Buddha. 551 Birth of Confucius. 320–184 Mauryan dynasty rules northern India. 273–232 Asoka introduces Buddhism into southern India. 221 Ch'in dynasty begins rule in China. 214 Great Wall of China completed. 206 Han Dynasty begins rule in China. **A.D.** 50B.C.–A.D.50 Buddhism introduced into China. 220–581 Civil war in China (Six dynasties period). 320–500 Gupta dynasty rules northern India. 360–390 Japanese conquer Korea.	**B.C.** *c.*40,000 First people migrate to America. *c.*15,000 Cave art practiced in Brazil. *c.*9000–7000 Flint arrowheads ("Folsom points") made in southern U.S.A. *c.*4500 Farming develops in central America. 3372 First date in Mayan calendar. *c.*1500 Stone temples built in Mesoamerica. *c.*1100–800 Olmec civilization flourishes in Mesoamerica. *c.*1000 Chavín people of Peru begin making pottery. *c.*700 Stone city of Chavín de Huántar built. *c.*500 Gallinazo and Salinar cultures flourish in Peru. **AD** *c.*200 Hopewell Indians build burial mounds in Ohio. *c.*300 Rise of Mayan civilization of Mesoamerica. *c.*500 Inuit begin hunting seals and whales.	**B.C.** *c.*50,000 First Aborigines arrive in Greater Australia. *c.*2000 First settlers arrive in New Guinea. *c.*1300 First settlers arrive in Fiji, Tonga, and Samoa. **A.D.** *c.*300 First settlers arrive in Polynesia.

**Europe**	**The Middle East**	**Africa**
452 Attila the Hun enters Italy. **455** Rome sacked by the Vandals. **476** The last Roman emperor is overthrown. **527–65** Justinian attempts to recover the old Roman Empire for the Byzantine Empire. **711** Muslims invade Spain. **732** Muslim armies defeated in France at Poitiers. ***c.*750** The feudal system starts to emerge. **771–814** Charlemagne rules vast Frankish Empire in western Europe. **793** Vikings start to raid Britain and then France. **843, 870** Charlemagne's empire split into three parts. **962** Otto I of Germany is crowned as the first Holy Roman Emperor. **1066** Normans invade and conquer England. **1154** Angevin Empire of England and France reaches its greatest extent. **1237** Mongols invade Russia, Hungary, and Poland. **1241** Hamburg and Lübeck set up a trading association, leading to the formation of the Hanseatic League. **1337–1453** Hundred Years' War between England and France. **1347–53** Black Death sweeps Europe.	**484** The Huns attack Persia and kill the emperor. **527–65** Under Justinian, the Byzantine Empire conquers much of the Middle East. **579** At the end of the reign of Chosroes I, the Sassanian Empire of Persia reaches its greatest extent. **622** Muhammad flees from Mecca to Medina. **630** Muhammad returns to Mecca and makes it the capital of his new empire. **632** Death of Muhammad and the start of Arab expansion throughout the Middle East. **642** The Arabs conquer Persia and overthrow the Sassanian Empire. **756** The Islamic Empire starts to break up into independent countries. **762** Baghdad is founded by al-Mansur. **971** World's first university is founded in Cairo. **1096–99** The First Crusade captures Jerusalem and establishes a number of Christian states in the area. **1187** Jerusalem is recaptured from the Crusaders. **1258** The Mongols capture Baghdad. **1261** The Mongol advance in the Middle East is stopped by the Egyptians. **1291** The Crusaders are finally thrown out of the Holy Land.	**400** Axum in Ethiopia converts to Christianity. **429** The Vandals overrun the Roman Empire in northern Africa and set up their own kingdom. **535** The Byzantine emperor Justinian conquers northern Africa. **639** Arabs invade Egypt. ***c.*700** Whole of northern Africa is now controlled by Arabs and converts to Islam. ***c.*700** Arab traders start to cross the Sahara and trade with the peoples to the south. **700–1200** Kingdom of Ghana, the first great African empire, grows rich on trade. **971** World's first university is founded in Cairo. **1071** East African ports of Kilwa and Gedi send ambassadors to China. **1235** The kingdom of Mali is established. ***c.*1250** The city of Djenné is founded. ***c.*1300** Great Zimbabwe emerges as a major trading empire. **1324** Mansa Musa, king of Mali, goes on a pilgrimage to Mecca and astounds everyone with his wealth. **1418, 1422** Chinese fleets visit East Africa in search of trade.

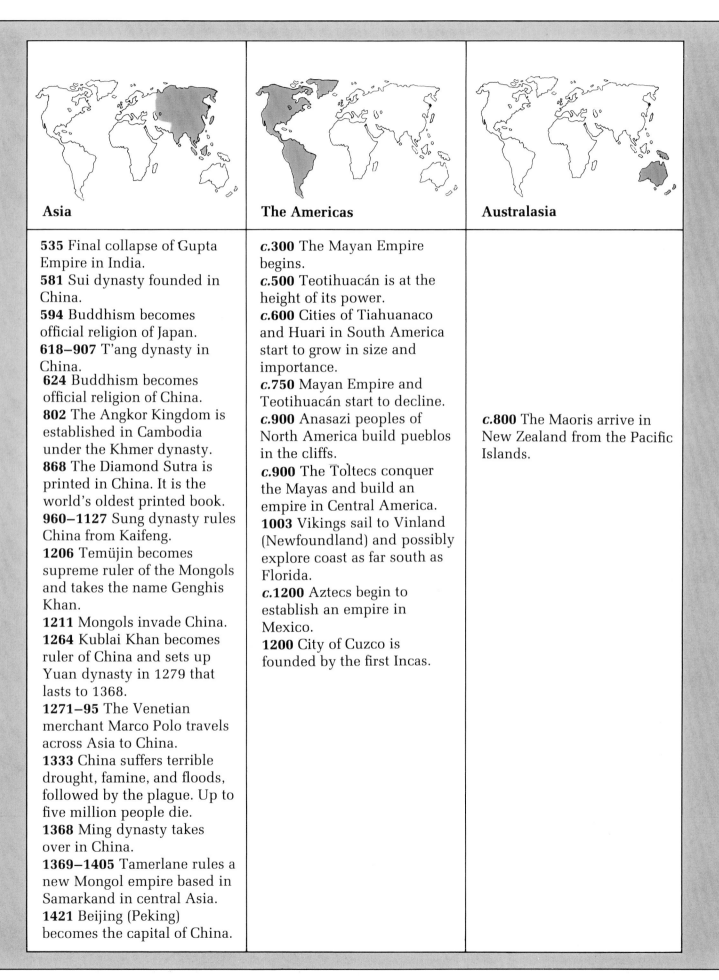

Asia

535 Final collapse of Gupta Empire in India.
581 Sui dynasty founded in China.
594 Buddhism becomes official religion of Japan.
618–907 T'ang dynasty in China.
624 Buddhism becomes official religion of China.
802 The Angkor Kingdom is established in Cambodia under the Khmer dynasty.
868 The Diamond Sutra is printed in China. It is the world's oldest printed book.
960–1127 Sung dynasty rules China from Kaifeng.
1206 Temüjin becomes supreme ruler of the Mongols and takes the name Genghis Khan.
1211 Mongols invade China.
1264 Kublai Khan becomes ruler of China and sets up Yuan dynasty in 1279 that lasts to 1368.
1271–95 The Venetian merchant Marco Polo travels across Asia to China.
1333 China suffers terrible drought, famine, and floods, followed by the plague. Up to five million people die.
1368 Ming dynasty takes over in China.
1369–1405 Tamerlane rules a new Mongol empire based in Samarkand in central Asia.
1421 Beijing (Peking) becomes the capital of China.

The Americas

*c.***300** The Mayan Empire begins.
*c.***500** Teotihuacán is at the height of its power.
*c.***600** Cities of Tiahuanaco and Huari in South America start to grow in size and importance.
*c.***750** Mayan Empire and Teotihuacán start to decline.
*c.***900** Anasazi peoples of North America build pueblos in the cliffs.
*c.***900** The Toltecs conquer the Mayas and build an empire in Central America.
1003 Vikings sail to Vinland (Newfoundland) and possibly explore coast as far south as Florida.
*c.***1200** Aztecs begin to establish an empire in Mexico.
1200 City of Cuzco is founded by the first Incas.

Australasia

*c.***800** The Maoris arrive in New Zealand from the Pacific Islands.

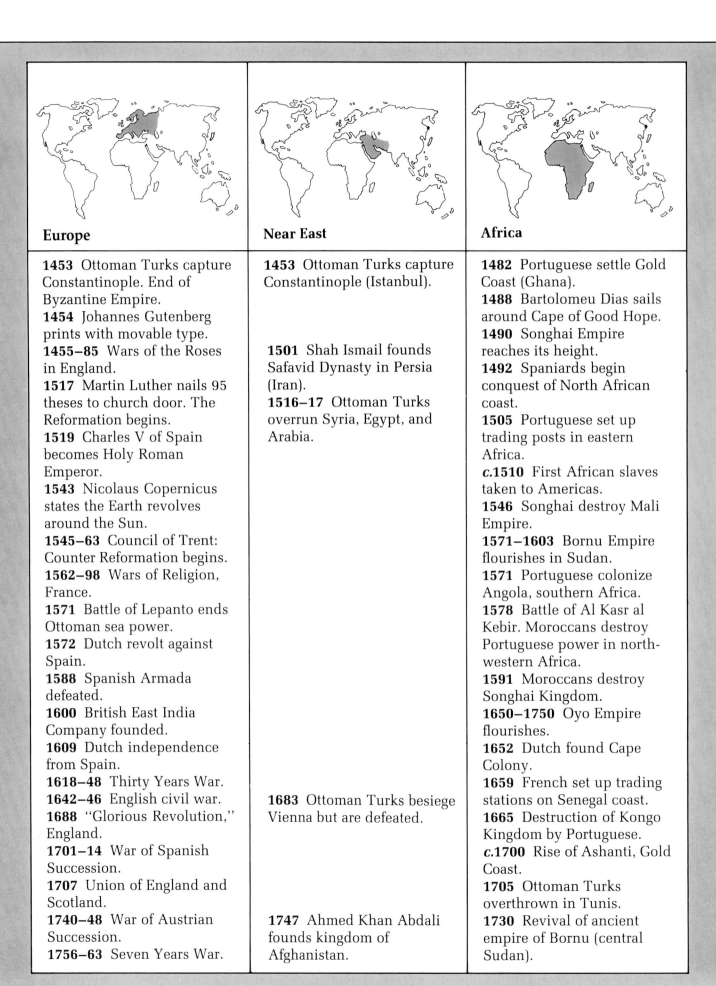

Europe

1453 Ottoman Turks capture Constantinople. End of Byzantine Empire.
1454 Johannes Gutenberg prints with movable type.
1455–85 Wars of the Roses in England.
1517 Martin Luther nails 95 theses to church door. The Reformation begins.
1519 Charles V of Spain becomes Holy Roman Emperor.
1543 Nicolaus Copernicus states the Earth revolves around the Sun.
1545–63 Council of Trent: Counter Reformation begins.
1562–98 Wars of Religion, France.
1571 Battle of Lepanto ends Ottoman sea power.
1572 Dutch revolt against Spain.
1588 Spanish Armada defeated.
1600 British East India Company founded.
1609 Dutch independence from Spain.
1618–48 Thirty Years War.
1642–46 English civil war.
1688 "Glorious Revolution," England.
1701–14 War of Spanish Succession.
1707 Union of England and Scotland.
1740–48 War of Austrian Succession.
1756–63 Seven Years War.

Near East

1453 Ottoman Turks capture Constantinople (Istanbul).

1501 Shah Ismail founds Safavid Dynasty in Persia (Iran).
1516–17 Ottoman Turks overrun Syria, Egypt, and Arabia.

1683 Ottoman Turks besiege Vienna but are defeated.

1747 Ahmed Khan Abdali founds kingdom of Afghanistan.

Africa

1482 Portuguese settle Gold Coast (Ghana).
1488 Bartolomeu Dias sails around Cape of Good Hope.
1490 Songhai Empire reaches its height.
1492 Spaniards begin conquest of North African coast.
1505 Portuguese set up trading posts in eastern Africa.
*c.***1510** First African slaves taken to Americas.
1546 Songhai destroy Mali Empire.
1571–1603 Bornu Empire flourishes in Sudan.
1571 Portuguese colonize Angola, southern Africa.
1578 Battle of Al Kasr al Kebir. Moroccans destroy Portuguese power in north-western Africa.
1591 Moroccans destroy Songhai Kingdom.
1650–1750 Oyo Empire flourishes.
1652 Dutch found Cape Colony.
1659 French set up trading stations on Senegal coast.
1665 Destruction of Kongo Kingdom by Portuguese.
*c.***1700** Rise of Ashanti, Gold Coast.
1705 Ottoman Turks overthrown in Tunis.
1730 Revival of ancient empire of Bornu (central Sudan).

Asia and the Far East	**The Americas**	**Australasia**

Asia and the Far East	The Americas	Australasia
1471 Vietnamese expand southward.	**1438** Inca Empire established, Peru.	
1498 Vasco da Gama reaches India via Cape of Good Hope.	**1440–69** Montezuma rules Aztec Empire.	
1519 Nanak founds Sikh religion in India.	**1492** Columbus reaches Caribbean.	
1526 Babur conquers Delhi and founds Mogul Empire.	**1494** Treaty of Tordesillas divides Americas between Portugal and Spain.	
1550 Mongol Altan Khan invades northern China.	**1497** Cabot reaches Newfoundland.	
1592–93, 1597–98 Japan invades Korea but is expelled by China.	**1520** Magellan crosses Pacific Ocean.	
*c.***1608** Tokugawa period begins in Japan.	**1521** Cortés conquers Aztec capital of Tenochtitlán.	
1608 Confucianism becomes official religion in Japan.	**1533** Pizarro conquers Peru.	
1619 Portuguese found Batavia (Jakarta).	**1545** Discovery of silver mines in Peru and Mexico.	
1630s Japan isolates itself from the rest of the world.	*c.***1560** Portuguese set up sugar plantations in Brazil.	
1644 Manchus found Ch'ing dynasty, China.	**1607** First English settlement in America (Jamestown, Virginia).	
1648 Taj Mahal completed, India.	**1608** French colonists found Quebec.	
1649 Russians reach Pacific and found Okhotsk.	**1620** Puritans on *Mayflower* land in New England.	
1690 Calcutta founded by British in India.	**1625** Dutch settle New Amsterdam.	
*c.***1690** Russia expands to Black Sea.	**1636** Harvard College founded—first university in America.	**1642** Tasman reaches New Zealand and Tasmania.
1697 Chinese occupy Outer Mongolia.	**1664** British seize New Amsterdam, rename it New York.	
1707 Death of Aurangzeb; decline of Mogul Empire.	**1682** La Salle explores Mississippi. Claims Louisiana for France.	
1708 Sikhs begin rule of Punjab.	**1728** Bering explores Alaska.	
1720 Manchus rule in Tibet.	**1759** British capture Quebec from French.	
1736 Nader Shah deposes Safavid dynasty.		**1768** James Cook explores Pacific.
1751 China overruns Tibet.		

Europe	**Near East**	**Africa**

1760s Industrial Revolution starts in Britain. **1762–96** Catherine the Great rules Russia. **1789** French Revolution begins. **1792** French declare republic; king is executed in 1793. **1799** Napoleon takes power in France. **1815** Napoleon defeated by British at Waterloo. The French monarchy is restored. **1848** Revolutions break out across Europe. **1861–70** Italy is united. **1870** France becomes a republic. **1914–18** World War I. **1917** Russian Revolution. **1919** Treaty of Versailles establishes new countries in Eastern Europe. **1922** Ireland becomes independent from Britain. **1933** Hitler takes power in Germany. **1936–39** Spanish civil war. **1939–45** World War II. **1940s** Communist governments take power in Eastern Europe. **1949** NATO and Warsaw Pact established. **1957** Treaty of Rome. **1968** Russian troops invade Czechoslovakia. **1989** Popular pro-democracy uprisings throughout Eastern Europe.	**1760** Ottoman Turks rule most of Near East. **1820** Britain establishes control in Persian Gulf states. **1908** Revolution in Turkey. **1914–18** World War I. **1917** Britain issues Balfour Declaration promising a Jewish homeland in Palestine. **1918** Ottoman Empire collapses: Iraq becomes independent. **1922** Syria and Lebanon under French control, Palestine and Jordan under British control. **1923** Turkish republic established under Kemal Atatürk. **1932** Saudi Arabia united. **1939–45** World War II. **1947–48** Palestine is partitioned, and the Jewish state of Israel is established. **1948** Arab–Israeli War. **1956** Egyptian take-over of Suez Canal leads to Israeli invasion and British–French occupation of Canal. **1967** Six Day Arab–Israeli War. **1973** Yom Kippur Arab–Israeli War. **1975** Civil war in Lebanon. **1979** Peace Treaty between Egypt and Israel signed. **1980–88** Iran–Iraq War. **1990** Iraq invades Kuwait—the Gulf War.	**1814** Britain acquires Cape of Good Hope from the Dutch. **1822** U.S. establishes Liberia as an independent state for freed slaves. **1830** France invades Algeria and starts to acquire North African empire. **1835–37** Dutch settlers (Boers) leave Cape Colony in Great Trek inland. **1842–43** War between Boers and British. **1869** Suez Canal opened. **1880s** Africa divided up by European powers. **1899–1902** Boer War between British and Boers leads to British domination of South Africa. **1910** South Africa becomes independent state in British Empire. **1914–18** World War I. **1935** Italy invades Ethiopia. **1939–45** World War II. **1954–62** Civil war in Algeria leads to French withdrawal. **1957** Ghana receives its independence from Britain. **1960** French African colonies become independent. **1975** Portugal declares all its African colonies independent. **1980** Zimbabwe is the last British colony in Africa to receive its independence. **1989** Open elections in Namibia, southwest Africa. **1990** Beginnings of an ease in apartheid in South Africa.

 **Asia**	 **The Americas**	 **Australasia**

Asia	The Americas	Australasia
1765 Britain establishes control over India. **1839–42** Trade War between China and Britain. **1854** U.S. forces Japan to trade with foreigners. **1857–58** Indian Mutiny against British rule. **1861** France establishes first colonies in Indochina. **1868** Japan starts to modernize. **1898–1900** Boxer Rebellion against foreign influence in China. **1904–5** Russo–Japanese War; Japan controls Korea. **1911** Chinese Revolution leads to overthrow of Manchu dynasty and establishment of republic. **1914–18** World War I. **1927** Chinese civil war begins. **1931** Japan begins conquest of China. **1939–45** World War II. **1946–54** War against French control of Indochina. **1947** India and Pakistan gain independence from Britain. **1949** Dutch grant independence to Indonesia. **1949** Communist Party takes control in China. **1950–53** Korean War. **1957–73** Vietnam War leads to union of Vietnam in 1975. **1989** Pro-democracy movement in Beijing, China, is severely repressed.	**1763** Britain gains complete control of Canada; acquires other colonies in America. **1775–83** American Revolution. **1776** American colonies declare their independence. **1783** United States formed. **1789** George Washington is first president of U.S.A. **1804** Haiti becomes independent after successful slave revolt. **1808–25** Spanish and Portuguese colonies in South and Central America fight for their independence. **1861–65** U.S. Civil War. **1867** Alaska is bought by U.S. from Russia. **1867** Canada becomes independent from Britain. **1869** Railroad link across U.S. **1914** Panama Canal opens. **1917** U.S. declares war on Germany. **1929** U.S. stock market crash leads to Great Depression. **1933–45** F. D. Roosevelt becomes president. **1941** U.S. enters World War II. **1945** United Nations Organization founded. **1963** President John F. Kennedy assassinated. **1968** Civil rights leader Martin Luther King, Jr. assassinated. **1987** U.S. signs INF Treaty with Soviet Union.	**1768–79** Captain Cook explores the South Pacific and claims Australia for Britain. **1788** The first convicts arrive in Australia from Britain. **1840** New Zealand becomes a British colony. **1880s** British, French, and Germans colonize South Pacific. **1900** Hawaii becomes a U.S. colony. **1901** Australia becomes an independent state in the British Empire. **1907** New Zealand becomes an independent state in the British Empire. **1914–18** World War I. **1920** Australia and Japan acquire former German colonies in the Pacific. **1927** Canberra becomes the federal capital of Australia. **1939–45** World War II. **1941** Japanese bomb naval base at Pearl Harbor, Hawaii, bringing U.S. into World War II. **1959** Hawaii becomes 50th state. **1970s** Many British island colonies in South Pacific receive their independence. **1975** Papua New Guinea receives its independence from Australia. **1985** South Pacific Forum draws up the South Pacific Nuclear Free Zone Treaty.

Index

Acknowledgments

The publishers wish to thank the following for supplying photographs for this
book:

Ancient Art and Architecture Collection 13, 17 (bottom), 29 (bottom), 34 (bottom)'
36 (middle and bottom), 76 (top), 88; Ashmolean Museum 58; Associated Press
139 (bottom right), 140 (bottom), 141 (bottom right), 142, 143 (left); Band Aid 144
(middle); The Bettmann Archive 123 (right); Bibliothèque Nationale 48 Ms Lat
4825 f37v; Bodleian Library 53 (top) Ms Marsh 144f.61; (left) Ms Lococke 37s
f3v4r, 63 Ms Douce 195 fol. 7, 68 (bottom) Ms Bodley 264 fol. 237, 93 (top left);
Bridgeman Art Library 118, 119 (left); British Library 72 (top), Ms Add 27695 fol.
8, 75 (top), 98 (bottom), 110 (top), 116 (top); British Museum 22, 43, 52 (middle),
68 (top), 85 (bottom), 97 (top right), 100 (top right); Camera Press 135 (left), 137,
138; Ekdotike Athenon 33 (left), Mary Evans Picture Library 93, 99 (bottom), 105
(bottom), 109 (bottom left), 115 (middle), 117, 119 (right), 121 (right), 122 (right),
123 (left), 127 (bottom), 128 (bottom), 130, 131 (left); Fitzwilliam Museum,
Cambridge 19 (bottom); Fotomas Index 106 (top and bottom), 108, 110 (bottom);
Courtesy, French Government Tourist Office 12; Giraudon 75 (bottom), 104
(bottom); Grisewood and Dempsey Ltd 121 (bottom); Sonia Halliday Photographs
14 (top), 15, 23 (top), 30, 36 (top), 37, 45, 49, 57, 62, 93 (top right); Robert Harding
Picture Library 55 (top), Barbara Heller 67 (bottom); Michael Holford 10 (bottom),
19 (top right), 27, 33 (right), 34 (top), 35 (right), 47, 60 (top), 65 (bottom), 77, 80,
82, 95 (bottom left), 106 (middle), 109 (top); Hulton-Deutsch Collection 101, 109
(bottom right), 127 (top); Hulton-Deutsch Collection 115 (bottom right), 122, 123
(bottom), 125, 129 (top), 134 (bottom), 135 (top); The Hutchison Library 10 (top),
23 (bottom), 25, 35 (left), 38 (top), 41, 42; 54, 67, 69, 79, 139 (bottom left), 141
(middle), 143 (right), 144 (top); ICCE Photolibrary/Mark Boulton 144 (bottom); The
Imperial War Museum 132, 136; The David King Collection 133 (bottom), 140
(top); The Kobal Collection 134 (top); The Library of Congress 124; The Mansell
Collection 55 (right), 70, 73 (top), 74, 81, 87, 89 (bottom), 98 (top), 103 (bottom),
120, 128 (top), 131 (right); Museum of Athens 32 (top), Museum of the American
Indian, Heye Foundation 39 (top); NASA 39 (middle left); NRSC Library 111, 129
(middle right); National Bibliothek, Vienna 9, 72 (bottom), 73 (bottom); National
Maritime Museum 86 (bottom); Peter Newark's Pictures 85 (top), 97 (top left and
bottom), 99 (right), 100 (top left), 116 (bottom), 135 (right); Novosti 133 (top);
Picturepoint 105 (top); Popperfoto 141 (bottom left); Punch Library 126; Ann
Ronan Picture Library 103 (top), 121 (left); SCALA 46, 50, 71; Courtesy, Sir John
Soane's Museum 61; Society for Cultural Relations with U.S.S.R. 139 (top); South
American Pictures 65 (top), 84; Spectrum Colour Library 19 (top left), 26, 32
(bottom); Straatliche Museum, Berlin 14 (bottom); Trinity College, Cambridge 51
(left); Trinity College, Dublin 51 (right), Universitets Oldsaksamlung 59 (right);
Vienna Art History Museum 90; The Wallace Collection 104 (top); Werner Forman
Archive 38 (top), 39 (bottom), 53 (right), 59 (left), 76 (bottom), 86 (top), 95 (top),
100 (bottom); ZEFA 17 (top), 29 (top), 52 (top), 55 (left), 64, 66, 89 (top), 93
(bottom), 94, 95 (bottom right), 107, 141 (top).